Blessed to Follow

Other books in the Lutheran Voices series

Blessed to Follow

The Beatitudes as a Compass for Discipleship

Martha E. Stortz

Augsburg Fortress

Minneapolis

In memory of William C. Spohn (1944-2005)

Take Lord, receive all my liberty, my memory,
my understanding, all my will,
All that I have, all that I possess, Lord, You have given all to me.
Now I give it back to you. All is yours.
Give me only your love and your grace. These are enough for me.

—Prayer of Ignatius of Loyola

BLESSED TO FOLLOW
The Beautitudes as a Compass for Discipleship

Copyright © 2008 Augsburg Fortress. All rights reserved. Except for brief quotations in critical articles or reviews, no part of this book may be reproduced in any manner without prior written permission from the publisher. For more information, visit: www.augsburgfortress.org/copyrights or write to: Permissions, Augsburg Fortress, Box 1209, Minneapolis, MN 55440-1209.

Scripture quotations, unless otherwise marked, are from the *New Revised Standard Version Bible*, copyright © 1989 by the Division of Christian Education of the National Council of Churches of Christ in the USA. Used by permission. All rights reserved.

This book is based on studies Martha Stortz wrote for the *Lutheran Woman Today* Bible Study, September 2007-June 2008. Copyright © Women of the Evangelical Lutheran Church in America. Used by permission.

Cover Photo © Frank Krahmer / Getty Images.

Library of Congress Cataloging-in-Publication Data
Stortz, Martha Ellen, 1952–
Blessed to follow: the Beatitudes as a compass for discipleship / Martha E. Stortz.
    p. cm. —(Lutheran voices)
Includes bibliographical references.
ISBN 978-0-8066-8007-1 (alk. paper)
1. Beatitudes. I. Title.
BT382.S78 2008
241.5'3—dc22   2007036811

Purchases of ten or more copies of this book are available at a discount from the publisher. For more information, contact the sales department at Augsburg Fortress, Publishers, 1-800-328-4648, or write to: Sales Director, Augsburg Fortress, Publishers, Box 1209, Minneapolis, MN 55440-1209.

The paper used in this publication meets the minimum requirements of American National Standard for Information Sciences—Permanence of Paper for Printed Library Materials, ANSI Z329.48-1984.
Manufactured in the U.S.A.

12   11   10   09   2   3   4   5   6   7   8   9   10

Contents

Introduction

Called by Blessing

"Come and get it!" The call rang out through the neighborhood every evening at six with such regularity that we could set our clocks by it. From swing sets and soccer games, the Cadigan children came scrambling. "Be here, or it will be gone!" For a family of six children, this was less a threat than a statement of fact. "Dinner's on the table!"

I grew up in one of Baltimore's fabled brick row houses, every one of them teeming with kids. The Cadigans had more kids than most, and Mrs. Cadigan corralled them with a lot of love and a loud voice. She shouted out orders like a drill sergeant. When provoked, her language was colorful and her threats ever more creative. The kids always showed up; they just wanted to hear what she would come up with next.

Jesus has a different way of getting people to the table. He does not resort to commands or threats. He simply blesses. The first word out of his mouth as he inaugurates his public ministry in Matthew's Gospel is *blessed*. And, if the disciples do not get it the first time, he repeats the word—not once, but nine times in all. Blessings roll down upon the crowd like water in a desert. As the people soak them in, the kingdom of God comes into their midst.

In a world according to God, blessings rule. Once our ears are tuned to the frequency of blessings, we hear them everywhere—like a song you can't get out of your head. Blessings are found throughout the Bible. As we become trained to see them in Scripture, we begin to trace the telltale path of blessings in our own lives. Here is what we find: (1) God calls us by blessing; (2) we call God by blessing; and (3) blessings leak.

God Calls Us by Blessing

Certainly *command* is not foreign to the vocabulary of God. The commands "You shall" and "You shall not" undoubtedly direct disciples in a certain way of life. Blessings, however, commission them, calling them into the path of discipleship to begin with.

Consider, for example, what Mary heard from her relative Elizabeth when she showed up on Elizabeth's doorstep confused, pregnant, and expecting rejection: "Blessed are you among women, and blessed is the fruit of your womb" (Luke 1:42). These words of blessing call Mary to a new vocation. She is "mother of the Lord," "God-bearer," or *theotokos* in the lyrical Greek of the ancient church.

Now, listen to the first sermon of Jesus' public ministry as he calls out his followers: "Blessed are the poor in spirit. . . . Blessed are those who mourn. . . . Blessed are the meek" (Matthew 5:3-5). With these words Jesus calls his followers to a way of understanding that runs contrary to conventional wisdom. God calls by blessing.

We Call God by Blessing

Blessing is also a way of getting God's attention. The psalmist knew this better than anyone: "Bless the LORD, O my soul, and all that is within me, bless his holy name" (Psalm 103:1). Blessings abound in these songs. This is most evident in the psalms of praise, but it is also true in psalms of lament and penance.

Since we are hardwired to praise the one who made us, we find blessing to be the heart's first language. Hear it in the ancient Hebrew prayers: "Blessed are you, O Lord God, King of the universe!" Listen to the words of Zechariah, Elizabeth's husband. When his tongue is unbound, the first words he utters are words of blessing: "Blessed be the Lord God of Israel, for he has looked favorably on his people and redeemed them" (Luke 1:68).

Blessing and calling mark our liturgy of baptism, the rite by which we are each called out to be disciples. We ourselves call out to God with the words "Blessed be God, the source of all life, the word of salvation, the spirit of mercy." Accordingly, we call out new Christians with words of blessing: "Child of God . . . you belong to Christ." In the world according to God, everything begins and ends with blessing.

Blessings Leak

Blessings are hard to contain. Like syrup at a boisterous Saturday morning pancake breakfast that manages to get all over everything—hands and feet, clothes and tablecloths, hair and chairs—blessings are messy. They are God's lavish way of reaching out to the whole of creation.

Hear the reach of divine blessing in the rest of Zechariah's song in Luke. A stunned crowd wonders "What then will this child become?" (1:66), and Zechariah tells them outright. "And you, child, will be called the prophet of the Most High" (1:76). Zechariah had begun by blessing "the Lord God of Israel" (1:68), but within a few verses, the blessings have spilled out all over the infant John, who will "go before the Lord to prepare his ways" (1:76). The blessings will not stop there either: John will bless people with the news that the kingdom of God is at hand.

Finally, hear these blessings come full circle in Jesus' ministry. In his first sermon, he calls out disciples by blessing them. In his last sermon, the Great Judgment (Matthew 25:31-46), he shows the same disciples how they have blessed him: "Come, you that are *blessed* by my Father, inherit the kingdom prepared for you from the foundation of the world; for *I* was hungry and you gave me food, *I* was thirsty and you gave me something to drink" (italics added). The ones blessed in the beginning of Jesus' ministry have become the blessing.

Blessings leak, and as we receive the blessings of Jesus' beatitudes, we become a blessing to others. The arc of Christian discipleship falls between Jesus' first and last sermons. Like a rainbow stretching across a strange and wonderful landscape, these blessings bear the promise of the world according to God. In this book, we listen with fresh ears to Jesus' first sermon, tuning our ears to the frequency of blessings. In doing so, we join disciples from across the centuries and around the world.

Historical Background

The beatitudes have a rich history of interpretation in the church, particularly for Lutherans. Not just the beatitudes, but the entire Sermon on the Mount was a sticking point for Martin Luther, and rightly so. By the late Middle Ages, these inaugural blessings had limited reach. The discipleship outlined in these blessings, and the costly grace therein, applied only to those in religious life, that is monks, nuns, and priests who had dedicated their lives to Christ. They were the only Christians considered eligible. They were the only Christians deemed "holy" enough to practice the discipleship embedded in blessing.

So, too, the perceived holiness of men and women in religious life qualified them, and them alone, to be addressed by the "You shall" commandments. Together with the beatitudes, these "You shall" commandments (one, three, and four) constituted "counsels of perfection" for the "perfect." The best that the laity could hope to do was abide by the "You shall not" commandments of the Decalogue, which are "You shall not kill," "You shall not steal," "You shall not commit adultery," and so on. The expectations were high for those in religious life because they were seen to have achieved the grace to comply, while the rest of us tried not to mess up too badly.

Such a two-story morality—a high moral bar for the spiritually elite and a lower bar for the rank-and-file disciples—was anathema to Luther. You could say that he demolished this two-story morality and put in a ranch house instead. Everyone is on one floor. It would probably be more accurate to say that he put in a huge staircase, invited everyone upstairs, and closed down the first floor. This is evident in his interpretation of the Ten Commandments in the Small Catechism. Every single "You shall not" commandment has been given a positive "You shall" interpretation. Just listen:

> *The Fifth Commandment: You shall not kill.* We should fear and love God, and so we should not endanger our neighbor's life, nor cause him any harm, but help and befriend him in every necessity of life.
>
> *The Sixth Commandment: You shall not commit adultery.* We should fear and love God, and so we should lead a chaste and pure life in word and deed, each one loving and honoring his wife or her husband.
>
> *The Seventh Commandment: You shall not steal.* We should fear and love God, and so we should not rob our neighbor of his money or property, nor bring them into our possession by dishonest trade or by dealing in shoddy wares, but help him to improve and protect his income and property.

The Eighth Commandment: You shall not bear false witness against your neighbor. We should fear and love God, and so we should not tell lies about our neighbor, nor betray, slander, or defame him, but should apologize for him, speak well of him, and interpret charitably all that he does.[1]

Maybe Luther's explanations for the Ten Commandments are so familiar to us that they no longer hold any surprises. But to a Christian in the late medieval period, his explanations would have been shocking. "Me? Outside the monastery, outside the convent?" Yes. Through baptism, we have all equally received the grace of Christ. We are all then equally enabled and graciously empowered to do what God requires.

Luther saw in the beatitudes a structure of command and promise. It is odd to think of the sayings "Blessed are the poor in spirit" and "Blessed are the pure in heart" as commands. But, Luther had been taught that the beatitudes were commandments and that they were applied to those athletes for Christ residing in monasteries and convents. They, and they alone, were the poor in spirit, the pure in heart, the merciful and the meek, the ones who mourned, and the ones hungering and thirsting for righteousness. Theirs, and theirs alone, were the promises attached to each commandment: "Theirs is the kingdom of heaven"; "They will see God"; and so on. Luther wanted to wrest the beatitudes away from the spiritually elite and make them the proud property of all disciples, and that is what he is trying to do in his study of the Sermon on the Mount and in his sermons on Jesus' first words.

Now, Matthew was not Luther's favorite Gospel; John held that honored post. Furthermore, Luther steadfastly distinguished between the gospel and the Gospels. In 1521, in *A Brief Instruction on What to Look for and Expect in the Gospels*, he wrote, "It is a common practice to number the Gospels and to name them by books and say that there are four Gospels." Then he went on: but, "one should realize that there is only one gospel, but that it is described by many apostles. Every single Epistle of Paul . . . is a gospel." "At its briefest," he wrote, "the gospel is a discourse about Christ, that He is the Son of God and became [hu-] man for us, that He died and was raised, that He has been established as a Lord over all things." Therefore, "just as there is no more than one Christ, so there is and may be no more than one gospel."[2] According to Luther, the books of the New Testament that preach the gospel best, in other words his canon within the canon, were John's Gospel, Paul's Epistles, especially his letter to the Romans, and 1 Peter. For Luther these were the "true kernel and marrow" of the New Testament.

Yet, even though Luther believed Matthew's Gospel paled next to John's on the doctrine of Christ, Luther judged Matthew "better than John" on the Christian life.[3] By this, he does not mean that disciples should think they can *earn* their salvation through these good works—far from it. Disciples have been *given* salvation through Christ. The beatitudes vividly describe the "fruit" of the indwelling Spirit of Christ that disciples have already received and to which they return again and again as they celebrate the Lord's Supper and return to their baptism.

In his distinctive teaching on the Christian life, Luther tried to steer a middle ground between Rome and the enthusiasts. On one hand, he hoped to avoid a monastic interpretation that hoarded these blessings for the spiritually elite, those in religious life. On the other hand, he hoped to avoid a theocratic interpretation that attempted to make the beatitudes a blueprint for political life. Instead, he planted the beatitudes firmly in the world. They were for all the baptized, specifically "Christians living in society," for, as he put it, Jesus "does not want the kind of saints that run away from human society." For "if I am in a desert, isolated from human society, it is no credit to me that I do not commit adultery or that I do not murder or steal. . . . For we are not made for fleeing human company, but for living in society and sharing good and evil."[4]

Despite the fact that Luther received his university degree in Scripture, specifically a *doctor in biblia,* throughout his life, he emphasized the priority of the spoken word rather than the written word. This spoken word was central to the life of the church and to the journey of discipleship. Indeed, he emphasized that "Christ did not command the apostles to write, but only to preach," and he fondly regarded the church itself "not as a pen-house, but a mouth-house," or *Mundhaus* in German.[5] So, while I am sure you can all read the beatitudes in the

Bible, I want you also to hear them, as if for the first time. Imagine that you are hearing them the way the crowd did. Imagine them being blessings to you. Imagine them blessing you even as you speak them.

Chapter Structure

As we work through Jesus' inaugural blessings, it is important to note that each chapter follows a similar pattern. First of all, these are targeted blessings, and they tap common human *experience*. They are not scattered randomly, nor are they simply cast into the wind. Rather, they are directed to people, more specifically to people in certain situations. The first four beatitudes target people in situations of suffering: those who are poor in spirit, deep in grief, meek, or persecuted for righteousness' sake. The second four beatitudes target people who help those who suffer: those who show mercy, make peace, display purity of heart, and fight for justice. To understand these targeted blessings, we need to identify places in our own lives where we have suffered or companioned those in suffering, and we will find ourselves blessed.

These blessings also bear stories. Each of these targeted blessings evokes a *biblical story* of one of our foremothers or forefathers in the faith: Hagar and Ishmael, Ruth the Moabite woman, Moses, and so on. Remembering these stories allows us to better understand the blessings.

Each blessing points to *Jesus*. In his first sermon, Jesus is the one blessing. By his last sermon, he shows that he is the one who is blessed. Each of the beatitudes directs us to a specific part of Jesus' story. As we remember his story, we learn more about what it means to follow him.

Each beatitude suggests a facet of *Christian discipleship*: the long-tempered character of biblical meekness, the heart's truest longing, and the spiritual poverty we cultivate so that God might fill us. These blessings fall on disciples, empowering us for a life of service, making us over into the kind of people Jesus calls us to be. The blessings get concrete.

Finally, each beatitude suggests a *practice* of discipleship: forgiveness, holy conversation, a soup kitchen, discernment, and so on. We may want to come up with additional practices, but the point is to root these blessings in the real world by living them. So in being blessed, we become a blessing to others.

1

Count Your Blessings; Hold Fast to the Promise

"Guess what the first words out of her mouth were?!" This shred of conversation, overheard as I hurried to my gate, intrigued me. As the plane lifted into the clouds, I reflected on the significance of first words. We cherish them like talismans; they promise to unlock a mystery.

In Matthew's Gospel, the Sermon on the Mount inaugurates Jesus' public ministry, and the first word out of Jesus' mouth is the word *blessed*. He repeats this word throughout his first sermon. In using the word *blessed*, Jesus reaches back to Old Testament stories of blessing in creation (Genesis 1:1—2:3) and in the call of Abraham (Genesis 12:1-3). At the same time, he reaches forward to his final sermon and the last words of his public ministry (Matthew 25:31-46). In both reaching back and moving forward, he encircles disciples in an embrace of blessing.

Jesus situates Christian discipleship squarely in the midst of blessing. As he speaks, he introduces himself to us, for he is both the one blessing and the one blessed. But he also introduces disciples to themselves, for the beatitudes offer a character sketch of who disciples will become if they follow Jesus. They function as a compass for the journey of Christian discipleship.

Echoes of Old Testament Blessing

As the saying goes, "Like father, like son," Jesus' first words echo those of the Creator. Genesis 1 shows the work of creation to be a shower of blessings. God surveys each day's work and blesses it. Indeed, if the Creation were a song, its refrain would be "And God saw that it was good" (Genesis 1:10, 12, 18, 21, 25).

Creation's blessings call order out of chaos, separating and distinguishing elements of the cosmos: light from darkness, earth from sea and sky, and sun from moon and stars. God blesses creation with a name and then passes the pleasure of naming on to Adam, and "whatever the man called every living creature, that was its name" (Genesis 2:19). God also assigns each of these newly named creatures a place to inhabit. There are creatures specially created to fly in the skies, to swim in the seas, and to crawl on the earth. Blessing knits a diverse creation together in a unity of peace.

The sheer persistence of divine blessing becomes clearest in the Fall. The incident with Satan and the fruit does not send creation careening back into the chaos from which it came. Divine blessings hold strong "against the rulers, against the authorities, against the cosmic powers of this present darkness, against the spiritual forces of evil in the heavenly places" (Ephesians 6:12). Nor can blessings be revoked, as we see so painfully with Jacob, who tricks his way into a paternal blessing intended for his brother Esau (Genesis 27). The Fall dissolves the peace of creation, leaving conflict in its wake. Humans are set against the earth and all its creatures and even against the work of their hands. Woman is set against man and child, with man against woman and the serpent against the other animals. Finally, God condemns the serpent to crawling on the earth, suggesting that before the Fall it walked upright.

Yet, even the curses of Genesis 3 cannot *erase* the blessings of Genesis 1. All is not lost. The blessing of Abraham (Genesis 12:1-3; 22:16-18) repeats and amplifies creation's blessings. Again, God calls order out of chaos, sending Abraham on a journey. God gives no destination, only a promise that "I will . . . make your name great." Not only does God bless Abraham, but also God makes him a blessing to others. After the near-sacrifice of Isaac, who is Abraham's only shot at establishing a lineage in the Hebrew world, God reiterates the promise: "And by your offspring shall all the nations of the earth gain blessing" (Genesis 22:18). Against all odds, Abraham's blessing extends through him and his offspring across the centuries and around the world, showing that Old Testament blessings leak.

Old Testament curses prove leaky as well. God tells Abraham that "the one who curses you I will curse" (Genesis 12:3), words that recur throughout the Old Testament. The threat reflects conventional wisdom to return evil for evil, "an eye for an eye," but Christians are counseled otherwise. Jesus himself directs disciples to "love your enemies and pray for those who persecute you" (Matthew 5:44), reversing the strict reciprocity of the ancient world. The apostle Paul continues the theme, reminding Corinthian Christians that Christ Jesus turned the old order upside down: "When reviled, we bless; when persecuted, we endure; when slandered, we speak kindly" (1 Corinthians 4:12-13). Paul's counsel sounds a lot like the beatitudes. Blessing replaces cursing as the Christian response in good fortune and in bad.

First Words: Jesus Blesses

Given the scope of biblical blessing, it is not surprising that Jesus begins his ministry with blessing. Yet, there is something both holy and terrifying about Jesus' blessings. Those he blesses are not in sought-after states of being. People would prefer to be "healthy, wealthy, and wise," as Benjamin Franklin described colonial American family values. But mourning, meekness, poverty, and persecution—not on your life! If Jesus were recruiting, these blessings would not move people to sign up. Yet, the words accurately describe the lives of too many of the world's peoples. Sorrow and oppression, hunger and thirst, persecution everywhere: the realities overwhelm us. This is where people are—too many people.

Jesus begins by blessing people where they are in life. And look at what happens to them. Each blessing is followed by a promise, and the promise reverses the condition of suffering in which Jesus finds people.

- Those who are called "poor in spirit," presumably lacking in spiritual expertise, turn out to be the ones inheriting the realm of all spiritual gifts, the kingdom of heaven.
- Those who mourn will find comfort. Indeed, the one who blesses them sends his spirit to them, the Holy Spirit, the Comforter.

- The meek inherit the earth—not the powerful or the ones with the most toys. This blessing reaches back to Moses, regarded in the Old Testament as "very humble, more so than anyone else on the face of the earth" (Numbers 12:3). God refuses Moses entry into the promised land, but this beatitude promises that he will inherit the whole earth, not just the land "flowing with milk and honey."
- Those who hunger and thirst for righteousness will be satisfied, for the righteousness of God stands before them.
- In a foreshadowing of the Lord's Prayer, the merciful, those who show forgiveness, receive the forgiveness they show to others.
- The soundtrack for the next beatitude is Augustine's (354–430) astute observations that "Our heart is restless until it rests in you."[1]
- The pure in heart will see God because there are no restless desires blocking their view.
- The peacemakers will be called "children of God," not "wimps" or "doormats" or "resisters," because they already participate in the divine shalom.
- Finally, Jesus promises the kingdom of heaven to those who are persecuted by the kingdoms of this world.

Jesus outlines a wonderful world of reversals, and in his words, the promises begin the blessing. Jesus blesses us by sharing our lot and reversing it. Every beatitude plays out this script. A philosopher calls this sort of speech *performative speech* because the words themselves deliver the goods. A Christians calls this *incarnation.*

It is important to notice that Jesus does not promise we will never be afraid, but he calms our fears just as he calmed the stormy seas. Words he repeats throughout his ministry address anxieties of skittish disciples then and now: "Fear not" and "Be not afraid." The only words Jesus repeats more frequently are the words of invitation: "Follow me." With this invitation, Jesus calls us out of a chaos of our own creation into the abundant life of discipleship.

How do these blessings begin the promised reversal? By giving people hope. Hope is not, as the poet Emily Dickinson put it, "the thing with feathers." Biblical hope is not hope in some *thing*; that some desire will be met or some outcome reached. Biblical hope is hope in *someone*. You do not so much *have* this hope, as if it is the product of fierce focus or creative imagination or even deep faith. This kind of hope has *you*. The apostle Paul could not put it better than he does in his letter to the Colossians: "Christ in you, the hope of glory" (Colossians 1:27).

Last Words: Jesus as the One Blessed

A seasoned preacher once remarked, "You've got one good sermon in you; give it with gusto." Maybe Jesus overheard his advice. His final sermon in Matthew's Gospel (25:31-46) recalls his first sermon, but it also reveals that the one who blesses joins the ranks of the blessed. Traditionally known as the Great Judgment, the last words in Jesus' public ministry could also be called "Revisiting the Beatitudes" because here he reveals himself as one who hungers and thirsts, one who is meek and mournful, and one who is naked and sick and imprisoned. Repetition renders the message more powerful: "*I* was hungry . . . . *I* was thirsty. . . . *I* was a stranger. . . . *I* was naked. . . . *I* was sick" (Matthew 25:35-36; italics added).

Jesus' final sermon shows him joined in solidarity with those whom his first sermon blessed. Jesus not only feels people's pain, but also shares it, bearing their burden and finding in it blessing. His final words reveal him as the victim of the world's ways: he is hungry, naked, thirsty, imprisoned, sick, and a stranger. The prophet Isaiah foretold the transformation: "He has borne our infirmities and carried our diseases . . . . He was wounded for our transgressions, crushed for our iniquities; upon him was the punishment that made us whole, and by his bruises we are healed" (Isaiah 53:4-5). Jesus takes our curse into his body; we take his blessedness into ours.

A Character Sketch of Discipleship

A high school graduation speaker promised that citizenship was only "a diploma away." The class cutup—distracted and distracting— was nudged by a more serious student: "This is who you're going to be in a few minutes. Listen up." The beatitudes tell us who we are going to be, so we listen to this character sketch of Christian discipleship.

Here creation's pattern alters only slightly. The family resemblance between Father and Son is grafted onto the relationship between disciples and their Lord. As he sets his face toward Jerusalem, Jesus takes on the character of the ones he blesses. Jesus blesses by sharing our lot and then reversing it. He becomes the one who is poor in spirit, the one who mourns, the meek, the one who hungers and thirsts for righteousness. He takes the curse into his own body; yet, even as he absorbs abuse, he ministers. He is mercy made flesh, pure in heart, the Prince of Peace, the one who is persecuted for helping others (Matthew 5:7-11). Jesus blesses, and God reveals him to be the blessing intended for the whole of creation.

Like master, like disciples: Jesus' lot will be ours. If this seems scary, it's because it is. In *The Conversion on the Way to Damascus* and *The Crucifixion of Saint Peter* the Italian artist Caravaggio (1571–1610) painted terror on the faces of two key disciples. Hanging across from one another in a small side chapel in the church of Santa Maria del Popolo in Rome, the paintings stand as bookends of discipleship.[2] Gazing upon the terrified faces of Jesus' faithful followers, one can almost hear the raw fear in Peter's question to Jesus: "Look, we have left everything and followed you. What then will we have?" (Matthew 19:27; cf. Mark 10:28) Discipleship is not for the faint of heart. The blessings of Jesus' first and last sermons are less like entrance requirements than a realistic description of what disciples can expect along the way. If we follow Jesus, we will find *ourselves* hungry and thirsty, naked and imprisoned, poor in spirit, mournful, and meek.

But just as God called out the whole of creation and blessed it, so Jesus calls out a wild and crazy crew of disciples, blesses them, and turns them, in spite of themselves, into a blessing for others. Blessed by God, disciples deliver on the promise of Abraham, spreading peace to "all the families of the earth" (Genesis 12:3).

Praise as a Way of Numbering Our Days

We count calories. We count out the day's pills or vitamin supplements. We count down the days to vacation or the minutes until quitting time. Along with all these everyday countdowns, we have more serious systems of calculation. We count grudges; we keep track of slights. We count American, Afghani, and Iraqi casualties from the War on Terror. We count upticks and downturns in the stock market. We count a mounting national deficit and a growing trade imbalance.

When someone asks us, "How are you doing?", which measurement should we use? Should we respond in terms of how close we are to quitting time? Should we run through a list of our grudges? Counting market points or minutes left in the work day makes a huge difference. Suddenly the psalmist's plea carries a certain urgency: "Teach us to number our days aright" (Psalm 90:12, New International Version [NIV][3]).

In his first big public appearance in Matthew's Gospel, Jesus outlines a new math: counting blessings. The psalmist was convinced that if we could speak from the heart, the first words out of our mouths would be words of blessing: "O Lord, open my lips, and my mouth will declare your praise" (Psalm 51:15). For centuries, monks and nuns have gathered before breakfast to pray the first office of the day. After the long silence of sleep, these are the first words they speak into the new day. We also preserve these words in our services of morning prayer.

Think of the "first words" that come to mind when you awaken: a list of things to do, or a cloudburst of anxieties, aches, and pains. Try waking by counting your blessings, beginning with the fact that you find yourself in a new day. Try ending your day the same way. See how many blessings you can number in your day. Be blessed.

Questions for Reflection

1. How have your blessings shaped your life as a disciple? For example, perhaps you were blessed to grow up in a loving home. Has that shaped how you treat people today? Perhaps you were not. Has that made you determined to do things differently?

2. How have your blessings called you into a life of discipleship? Into certain relationships? Into a particular career or profession, or a particular role in your family or place of service?

3. How can blessing someone else bless you in return? Count the ways, the instances, and the people.

2

Poor in Spirit; Rich in Blessing

Blessed are the poor in spirit, for theirs is the kingdom of heaven.
—Matthew 5:3

"You'd give away the shirt off your back," one of the locker room buddies teased another. "But then you'd be arrested for creating a public disturbance." We took stock of Susan's ample frame and burst out laughing. Susan laughed loudest, being as generous with her laughter as she was with her clothes. As we got into our cars, Susan rumbled away in a wreck that had seen at least a decade on the road, while the rest of us hopped into the latest models that Detroit or Tokyo had to offer. Susan had fewer material goods than any of us. She rented a small apartment and lived on a teacher's salary, and we watched her bathing suits sag after seasons of use. Yet, Susan lived with an abundance that contrasted sharply with her friends' anxiety over making ends meet. She lived a life poor in material goods but rich in blessing. She acted like she had already inherited a piece of the kingdom, or in her case, the queen-dom.

Matthew's Gospel blesses "the poor in spirit," while Luke bluntly addresses "you who are poor" (Luke 6:20). Is there a difference? Scholars debate what kind of poverty is at stake in this beatitude: material or spiritual. Is Matthew qualifying Luke's clear commitment to physical poverty? If spiritual poverty is at stake, what does it mean anyway? Poverty, in any sense of the word, does not seem like much of a blessing. Yet, the promise of the "kingdom of heaven" describes a stunning reversal of earthly fortunes. The beatitude suggests generosity as the spiritual practice that invites us to live into its blessing: "Blessed are the poor in spirit, for theirs is the kingdom of heaven."

Possessed by Possessions

Trappers from the African jungle tell of capturing a rare and fragile species of monkey. They hollow out a gourd, insert a small hole in the side, and fill the gourd with peanuts. Then the trappers hang the gourds in trees and wait. Without fail, the monkeys come, reach into the gourd, grab a fistful of peanuts and find that their hands—now filled with peanuts—can no longer fit through the small hole. While the monkeys twist and turn to find a way out, the trappers return to bag them for export to zoos around the world.

Trappers know something that monkeys do not. They know that the monkeys will refuse to release their peanuts even under threat of capture. If they would only let go, they could run free. But the monkeys desperately hang onto those nuts, even as the trapper bags them.

Have we advanced that much beyond our primate cousins? A warning from Mount Sinai suggests that we have not. The first thing God wanted to impress upon the chosen people was how dangerous possessions were: "I am the LORD your God . . . you shall have no other gods before me" (Exodus 20:2-3). The commandment refers to the various gods and goddesses peoples of the ancient world worshiped. We fool ourselves into thinking idols are a thing of the past. If we rummage through our anxiety closets, we find plenty that threatens to enthrall us.

Martin Luther located these other gods by following our heart-strings: "That to which your heart clings and entrusts itself is . . . really your God."[1] Our possessions tug at us, and we stand toe-to-toe with the great biblical worrywarts: "Will thieves make off with my profit?" or "Will there be an uptick in the stock market or a downturn?" There are even questions with the trapping of spirituality: "Will people like me?" or "Do I spend enough time in prayer?" or "Is the glass half-empty or half-full most of the time?" God does not want us to waste time measuring. Anxiety turns the heart in on itself (*cor incurvatus in se*), transforming possessions into gods.

Jesus knew all too well the power of possessions to enthrall. For this reason, he opened his first sermon with the words "Blessed are the poor in spirit." He knew that people become possessed by their possessions. Indeed, the most graphic healings in the New Testament involve demonic possession. Jesus kicked out the demons inhabiting a Gerasene man, and the spirits moved into a herd of pigs, stampeding them into the sea (Mark 5:1-13). In casting out demons, Jesus literally re-possessed the man, claiming him as his rightful possession. By showing us *whose* we really are, these healing stories teach us *who* we really are. We are a people possessed!

When we gather in the name of the Father, Son, and Holy Spirit, we confess who rightly owns us. We testify to whom we rightfully belong. The apostle Paul put this new membership in words: "You belong to Christ, and Christ belongs to God" (1 Corinthians 3:23). Through baptism, we are grafted onto the body of Christ. Through him, we already set one foot into the kingdom of heaven. The only way to continue the journey is with open hands, ready to receive the gifts and the guidance offered to us.

Finding the Path with Open Hands

While praying in a congregation where I had never worshiped before, I was surprised to feel a hand on my shoulder. I opened my eyes and discovered that the practice of this community was to hold hands during the Lord's Prayer. Finding no hand to hold, my neighbor had simply laid her hand on my shoulder to include me. I quickly dug my hands out of my pockets, opened them to receive the hands of neighbors on both sides, and stepped into the circle of prayer.

No one can enter a circle of prayer with her hands buried deep in her pockets, and no one can give or receive anything with her hands clenched around her possessions. Martin Luther understood this. Two days before he died, he wrote a note that said: "We are all beggars."[2] This puzzled the people around him, but I suspect that Luther wanted to leave his friends with the image of open hands. Poverty loosens our hold on possessions, freeing us for the journey of discipleship.

We only enter the kingdom of heaven with open hands. As we journey, we sing the songs of our foremothers, Mary, the mother of Jesus, and Hannah, the mother of Samuel. Their songs tell stories of amazing reversal: the poor becoming rich, the lowly lifted up, and the mighty knocked from their thrones. These are songs of the kingdom of heaven, where God alone rules. And the songs come from the lips of women whose hands had been forced open by circumstance. They had nothing to cling to but God. As we listen, their songs become ours.

Mary's Song

As you read the Magnificat (Luke 1:46-55), put yourself in Mary's sandals. She is young, female, pregnant, unmarried, and adrift in a world that prizes a woman's chastity. She is engaged to be married to a man who knows the child she bears does not belong to him. The Gospel of Matthew tersely reports the situation: "Joseph, being a righteous man and unwilling to expose her to public disgrace, planned to dismiss her quietly" (Matthew 1:19). We can only imagine what Mary's future might have held.

At this point, the only person Mary had discussed her shocking situation with was an angel, and Gabriel was not particularly pastoral. But the angel did point her to her cousin Elizabeth, a relative who was also impossibly pregnant. Elizabeth offered Mary consolation, and that consolation came with words of blessing: "Blessed are you among women, and blessed is the fruit of your womb" (Luke 1:42). With open hands and open arms, Elizabeth embraced her kinswoman. Mary responded with praise to a God whose ways are as mysterious as they are gracious: "My soul magnifies the Lord."

Mary sang of how God reversed her fortune. Her "lowliness" became something "all generations will call . . . blessed." She moved from her situation to speak of all the "lowly," and her song sounds a lot like Jesus' first sermon. Mary uttered the beatitudes before Jesus was even born. The blessings of her pregnancy echo down through the centuries.

Hannah's Song

Mary's praise repeats an older song from another unlikely mother. Hannah was barren, a condition that brought ridicule and risk upon her. Women without children had no one to care for them in their old age. Children were the ancient world's social security net, the only hedge against starvation. The Old Testament makes a particular provision for widows. Landowners let them glean grain from the edges of the field. It was their only hope of survival.

Hannah turned her firstborn over to the Lord, consecrating him for service. But her legacy was more than her progeny, for she left behind the song that served as the model for Mary's Magnificat. Like the Magnificat, Hannah's song (1 Samuel 2:1-10) praises God and promises a reversal of fortune for all who trust in the Lord.[3]

Jesus: The King of Love

Both of these hymns of our foremothers present mirror images of a world where the rich get richer and the poor get poorer. The kingdom of heaven reverses people's fortunes, and Hannah's song praises its ruler:

> The LORD will judge the ends of the earth;
>> he will give strength to his king,
>> and exalt the power of his anointed. (1 Samuel 2:10b)

Jesus was not the kind of king people expected. Mark's Gospel (8:27-33) says it all. Jesus asked the disciples, "Who do people say that I am?" They reply "John the Baptist," "Elijah," and "one of the prophets." These answers must have troubled Jesus, for they replay his temptation in the wilderness (cf. Matthew 4:1-11; Mark 1:12-13; Luke 4:1-13), where he was tempted to turn stones into bread, to leap from the pinnacle of the temple, and to be king of all the earth. Elijah's appearance in the temple precincts preceded the day of salvation. Moses, the greatest of the prophets, brought food from heaven and water out of rocks. John the Baptist announced that the "kingdom of heaven has come near" (Matthew 3:2). When Jesus posed the question to those who knew him best, Peter responded with another wrong answer—at least in Mark's Gospel—the Messiah. In Jewish expectation, the Messiah would fight with military might to restore the promised land to the chosen people.

Jesus began to teach about a different kind of kingship, a "Son of Man" who would suffer, be rejected, be killed, and be raised from the dead (Mark 8:31). More importantly, he showed the disciples—then and now—that he is the one to whom all of the beatitudes point. The one who blesses is the same one who is poor in spirit and pure in heart, who mourns and makes peace, who is merciful and meek, and who is persecuted to death for his goodness.

Jesus' kingdom confounded people. Some like Peter wanted Jesus to be a military leader. Others could not stand his humility. Still others resisted that bright goodness. Matthew's Gospel highlights the kingdom; it spends a lot of face time with its king. The passion narrative, in particular, displays the confusion this kind of king created. More than any of the other Gospel accounts, Matthew's portrays a king's poverty. Jesus had no one to serve him and no one to save him. He faced death alone, a leader without followers and a king without servants. Listen to the taunts flung at Jesus from the crowd; imagine how they must have sounded to this King of Love.

- "This is Jesus, the King of the Jews" (27:37).
- "You who would destroy the temple and build it in three days, save yourself!" (27:40)
- "He saved others; he cannot save himself" (27:42).
- "He is the King of Israel; let him come down from the cross now, and we will believe in him" (27:42).
- "He trusts in God; let God deliver him now, if he wants to; for he said, 'I am God's Son'" (27:43).

If you have one of those Bibles with the words of Christ in red, look at how silent Jesus becomes as the Passion grinds to his death: the red lines become fewer and farther between. Jesus becomes more and more silent. He is poor even in speech. Matthew records Jesus' final, and only, words from the cross as "My God, my God, why have you forsaken me?" (27:46)

Yet, when Jesus returned as the risen Christ, he greets the disciples with the words "Do not be afraid" (Matthew 28:10). Love conquers death; the Spirit of God in Christ rescues us from the undertow of evil and from the burden of our possessions. In describing Jesus' kingship, a familiar hymn draws on Psalm 23. It is worth hearing against the back-drop of the beatitude being discussed: "The King of Love My Shepherd Is," written by Henry Baker.

Following a King of Love

What does it mean to serve this kind of king? As we have seen, the disciples hoped Jesus was the kind of king who would rise up with military might and reclaim the promised land for God's chosen people. Then they could be generals in the army of liberation. But if Jesus was the King of Love, what did this mean for them?

Peter put the question to Jesus directly: "Look, we have left every-thing and followed you. What then will we have?" (Matthew 19:27) Just prior to Peter's question, Jesus had ended a conversation with a rich young man, and he ended it abruptly. He issued the invitation to dis-cipleship: "Follow me" and the rich young man walked away (Matthew 19:16-22). The man surely had more possessions than the whole lot of disciples put together. In addition, he knew the law to the letter. One thing he did not know, however, which turned out to be the one thing he needed most, was how to unburden himself from his possessions. He was a man possessed, and even Jesus could not cast out these demons.

The encounter left the disciples uneasy, prompting Peter's query. I bet Peter could have answered his own question. Jesus' lot will be theirs, and Peter realizes he is too far down the road of discipleship to turn back.

We are all in Peter's position. The apostle Paul offered a song to rally the troops. Corinth was one of the biggest and most important cities of the ancient world, and we imagine members of Paul's commu-nity to be urbane and sophisticated. They considered themselves "rich in spirit," and Paul struggled with some of the gifted and charismatic leaders among them. Laced with irony, Paul's words contrast the wealth and arrogance of people rich in spiritual and material gifts with the life of discipleship.

> For I think that God has exhibited us apostles as last of all, as though sentenced to death, because we have become a spectacle to the world, to angels and to mortals.

We are fools for the sake of Christ,
    but you are wise in Christ.
We are weak,
     but you are strong.
You are held in honor,
    but we in disrepute.
To the present hour we are hungry and thirsty,
    we are poorly clothed and beaten and homeless,
        and we grow weary from the work of our own hands.
When reviled,
    we bless;
when persecuted,
    we endure;
when slandered,
    we speak kindly.
We have become like the rubbish of the world, the dregs of all things,
to this very day. (1 Corinthians 4:9-13)

Paul closed with a rhetorical question that revealed his affection for the community: "Am I to come to you with a stick, or with love in a spirit of gentleness?" (1 Corinthians 4:21) The answer would have been obvious to the Corinthians. After all, this was their beloved teacher. He came to them always with love. This is what it means to follow a King of Love.

Freedom through Generosity

An old preacher exhorted his congregation: "I want you to give 'til it hurts. And then, I want you to give until it stops hurting!" After listening to this man Sunday after Sunday, these folks would get used to diving into their pockets. After a while, they would think nothing of it. By then, the preacher's command would be a disposition etched deeply on their hearts. Generosity is God's way of unclenching our hands, freeing us from our possessions.

Think back on Susan, the woman who would give you the shirt off her back. She may have been generous to a fault, but I suspect Jesus had Susan in mind when he said, "To all those who have, more will be given, and they will have an abundance; but from those who have nothing, even what they have will be taken away" (Matthew 25:29). Jesus is not making a divine prediction; rather, he states a simple fact: a generous person feels overwhelmed with abundance. She is free to share her possessions. In contrast, the ungenerous person feels underwhelmed with what she has. In her mind, her possessions are under constant siege. She lives in a state of scarcity, and she hoards what little she has, lest "even what she has be taken away."

Generosity is the gift that keeps on giving. In seeing generosity as a practice of discipleship, we are freed *from* our possessions and freed *for* belonging to Christ.

Questions for Reflection

1. If your home was burning, the hill behind you was sliding, the floodwaters were rising, and you had to leave, what would you take? What would be in your hands?

2. Think of one incident in your own life that seemed a misfortune and turned into a blessing. Identify one reversal of fortune in your own life; remember how it started and how it turned out. Did you bless anyone or anything for the change? Did you see any patterns of the reversal of fortune after that?

For Further Reflection

Psalm 72

This psalm of affirmation and praise addresses the ruler of an earthly kingdom who brings all of his earthly possessions to bear on the plight of the poor and needy. Such generosity receives God's blessing, for in this the earthly ruler imitates the extravagant generosity of the heavenly ruler. The psalm ends with praise to the source of all blessing.

Few of us could lay claim to royalty with its rich trappings of power and wealth of possession. Still, we have all been blessed, and we all worship the source of all blessing. As you reflect on this psalm, think of how you might use your blessings to help the poor and needy. Then think of all the ways in which you yourself are poor and needy. Call to mind all the people who have blessed you, and give thanks to God for their generosity.

3

The Country of Mourning

Blessed are those who mourn, for they will be comforted.
—Matthew 5:4

After my husband, Bill, died, a colleague sent an extraordinary letter of comfort. It went like this: "My mother died of brain cancer, and I know the pain. I hope you have also had some funny and holy moments. I know that in heaven all the tears will be wiped away. Still, I'd like some answers."

Anyone who mourns also longs for the comfort of answers. Often the questions cannot even be put into words. My questions surprised even me. They were not questions like "Why him?" or the related "Why me?" Nor did I find myself asking the questions of prophets and psalms, "Why do the wicked prosper?"[1] or the more updated query "Why do bad things happen to good people?" The question that haunted me most was "What is he doing now?" When Bill was alive, I knew his every movement. As his caregiver, I had to know; as his wife, I wanted to. Now that he had joined the communion of saints, I could not locate him on any map. Along with the huge hole that his absence left behind, I mourned my own ignorance. How do the saints spend their days? This beatitude hints at the answer to this question: they offer blessing and comfort to those who mourn. As we remember them, they quite literally re-member us.

Into the Country of Mourning

Mourning is more a place than an emotional state, and no one chooses to go there. Loss dumps us into a wilderness of mourning, and we wander until we find our way out. There are no maps to the country of mourning, for each person's journey is different. Yet, the wanderer finds herself blessed with guides. We have two powerful biblical guides in the persons of Hagar and Mary.

29

Hagar in the Wilderness of Grief

The chapters of Genesis 11–25 recount the story of Abraham and Sarah, whose names God changes and whose childlessness God alters. Yet, another story breaks into this central narrative, and the story of Hagar and Ishmael is an important interruption. Reading their story whole respects the wilderness of Hagar's grief and also celebrates her comfort (Genesis 16:1-16; 17:18-23; 21:9-21). As we reconstruct the story of Hagar and Ishmael from the accounts scattered throughout the middle chapters of Genesis, we see that what begins in mourning ends in blessing.

Hagar and Ishmael find themselves in the wilderness twice in this story. Both times, they prepare to die. The first time (Genesis 16:1-16), Ishmael is growing in Hagar's womb. Sarai has expelled her from Abram's household, where she was impregnated by Abram at Sarai's command. Surely this counts as rape: the ancient world regarded servants as little more than property. Perhaps Sarai hoped to raise the child as her own, for her barrenness made her an object of shame. Perhaps Abram hoped for an heir, someone to fulfill God's promise that "a great nation" would rise from his loins. Whatever their hopes were, Hagar's wishes did not count. When she claimed the child as her own, Sarai interpreted her behavior as contempt. Abram did not protest when Sarai sent the pregnant servant away. Expulsion could have ended the story, for being banished into the wilderness was a death sentence.

What comfort could Hagar have hoped for in the wilderness of her grief? The angel's command for Hagar to return to her imperious mistress could not have been good news (16:9). Yet, the angel of the Lord comforts her with the knowledge that she will live and bear a son. More important, the angel blesses her with a name for the boy: Ishmael. Hagar receives all of this, and she offers a blessing and bestows a name in response. She names the Lord who spoke to her "El-roi." At the very site where she faced death, she saw God—and lived. Her story recalls Job's, another person thrust into the country of mourning: "I had heard of you by the hearing of the ear, but now my eye sees you" (Job 42:5).

Hagar and Ishmael find themselves in the wilderness a second time, again because of Sarah's jealousy (Genesis 21:9-21). Sarah herself has a new name, and the name indicates her new status. She has become a mother; she has borne Abraham a child, Isaac. Angry to see

Ishmael and Isaac treated as equals and anxious to keep God's promises all to herself and her own offspring, Sarah has Abraham banish Hagar and her son into the wilderness. This time, Hagar is certain of death for herself and her child. She cannot bear to watch her child die, and she sets the boy under the only shade she can find.

What comfort would Hagar hope for this time? If she hopes for a repeat of the angel's first performance, she will be disappointed. This time she will not see God. Instead, the angel points her to a well from which she and her son can drink. If she hopes to be returned to civilization, she will be disappointed. She and Ishmael make the wilderness their home, moving from oasis to oasis with the desert's seasons. Instead, God fulfils a promise made to Abraham and Hagar, for between Hagar's two exiles in the desert, Abraham found the courage to stick up for his illegitimate son (Genesis 17:18). In response to Abraham's plea for Ishmael's protection, God promises that Ishmael too will be blessed. From him a great nation is born, and that nation rises out of a place of death: the desert.

How does the story of Hagar's mourning comfort us? Four blessings come from the scattered story of this desert wanderer.

1. Comfort comes—but not always in ways we expect. God hears the cries of Hagar and Ishmael, and God answers them.
2. God's comfort is a little like a lightning strike: it never comes in the same way twice. God's first wilderness comfort comes through Hagar's submission to her grief, as God orders her back to the site of her oppression. God's second wilderness comfort comes when the wilderness becomes a home.
3. The wilderness of mourning is also a place where we see God—and live.
4. The wilderness can become a home and a place of blessing.

Mary in the Wilderness of Grief

Like Hagar's story, Mary's story falls outside the main spotlight. The Gospels focus on the life of Jesus; the life of his mother must be gathered from scattered accounts. She too faced the death of a child; she too watched death from a distance. While Hagar guarded Ishmael from an arrow's shot away, Mary stood at the foot of a cross. As life drained out of Jesus' body, she must have thought back on the prophecy of Simeon: "This child is destined for the falling and the rising of many in Israel, and to be a sign that will be opposed so that the inner thoughts of many will be revealed—and a sword will pierce your own soul too" (Luke 2:34-35).

The words must have terrified Mary and thrust her into a wilderness of foreboding. She mourned without quite knowing what to weep for. At the foot of the cross, as images from their life together unwound wildly before her eyes, Mary remembered always having that feeling of foreboding. She had always been waiting for the other shoe to drop; she had always been waiting for the sword to pierce her flesh. Now she felt it go deeper.

The grief of her tragedy made Mary into an icon of suffering for Spanish and Latin American spiritualities, the *mater dolorosa*, or "sorrowful mother." Particularly in cultures and centuries with high rates of infant mortality, the sorrowful mother took on huge significance. Images and statuaries feature Mary clad in black and weeping. I saw Mary's tears in the face of a young mother at her newborn child's deathbed. She looked like the air was being sucked out of her breath by breath. The two had been roommates: they had shared space in the house of her body for almost nine months. "I feel ripped apart," the mother said. When a beloved child, spouse, or partner dies, those who are left behind become amputees. For a long time, they have sensation in that missing limb: a flickering impulse from something that is no longer there.

Yet, Simeon's prophecy in Luke's Gospel was not only a warning. Simeon begins with blessing, and he blesses both of Jesus' parents. As we gather the story of Mary from its scattered sources throughout the Gospels, we find Simeon's blessing borne out in various ways. Mary occasioned Jesus' first miracle in the wedding at Cana, where he turned ordinary water into extraordinary wine (John 2:1-11). Then at the foot of the cross, Jesus blessed her with a surrogate son, as he blessed John with a surrogate mother. With this blessing, he entrusted the two people he loved most to each other (John 19:25-27). The knowledge that his mother would be well cared for gave Jesus permission to die. The Gospels do not name Mary as being present in any of the post-resurrection appearances of Jesus, but she prayed with the disciples after Jesus' ascension (Acts 1:14) and was presumably present for the descent of the Spirit, the Comforter, at Pentecost (Acts 2:1-4).

How does the story of Mary's mourning comfort us? Four blessings come from the scattered story of Jesus' mother.

1. Comfort comes when we listen for it. In her instructions to the servants at Cana, Mary leaves counsel for anyone looking for a path through the wilderness: "Do whatever he tells you" (John 2:5). We have no maps for the journey of discipleship, and the wilderness of mourning remains uncharted. But disciples follow a person, and to move forward, we need to listen for his voice.
2. Comfort comes disguised. As the wedding at Cana demonstrates, the ordinary elements of daily life bear God's extraordinary graces.
3. Loss opens us to new possibilities, as Jesus' death opened the door to a new relationship between Mary and the beloved disciple.
4. Jesus blesses us with his Spirit, the Holy Spirit, the Comforter. The Spirit of the risen Christ descended on the disciples at Pentecost and remains in the world for all time.

One Who Mourns; One Who Comforts

What is the shortest verse in the Bible? John 11:35. The King James Version (KJV) translation, "Jesus wept,"[2] packs a punch that is missing in the New Revised Standard Version (NRSV), "Jesus began to weep," but regardless of the translation, these words telegraph to us Jesus' humanity. Being Son of God and Ruler of the Universe could not spare him tears. Jesus wept at his dear friend Lazarus' death.

Jesus also responds to Martha's bold confession and Mary's tender tears with tears of his own. The passage is so familiar that we tend to skip over the drama. The scene reveals Martha as the first evangelist. She understands Jesus' true identity as no one else has, not even his closest friends, the disciples. Martha knows something that eludes the disciples: "Yes, Lord, I believe that you are the Messiah, the Son of God, the one coming into the world" (John 11:27). A little later, Mary's tears show the depth of Jesus' compassion. He knows Lazarus is dead, yet that fact has not brought him to tears. Rather, seeing Mary's grief draws out his own. "When Jesus saw her weeping, and the Jews who came with her also weeping, he was greatly disturbed in spirit and deeply moved" (11:33).

These were not the only tears Jesus shed. He wept over the fate of Jerusalem, uttering words that echo with import for that same city today: "If you, even you, had only recognized on this day the things that make for peace!" (Luke 19:42) Even then, Jerusalem fell under the judgment of war and faction. There were also tears in the garden of Gethsemane as Jesus waited for his time of trial. The Gospels record that Jesus was in anguish, "and his sweat became like great drops of blood falling down on the ground" (Luke 22:44; cf. Matthew 26:37-39).

Jesus' tears over the loss of a dear friend, the fate of a great city, and his own impending death establish his humanity. He knows the full range of human experience, and the comfort he offers comes from the depths of suffering.

When my husband, a former Roman Catholic priest, got married, one of his old high school buddies came up to him, clapped him on the back, and said, "Thanks for becoming one of us." Most of the boys in the St. Ignatius Preparatory School from the class of 1962 had been married for decades by that point, and my husband had been a steady support to those marriages and the children they produced. He had been through their ups and downs, as well as deaths and divorces, and now he was joining their ranks. He would know firsthand that strange and wonderful "country of marriage."[3]

Jesus became one of us to experience the full range of human experience: joy and sorrow, delight and mourning. I have no answers when people pose the ancient questions that always follow in the wake of tragedy: "Why me?", "Why him?", "Why do bad things happen to good people?", "Why do the wicked prosper?" No one does. Instead, I find myself thinking about that high school buddy: "Thanks for becoming one of us." Even God has no answers. God does not give an explanation for suffering; God gives us a Son so that God can experience everything the human condition has to dish out.

Because Jesus too has suffered, the comfort he offers to disciples across the centuries is real. As if he could already taste their tears, Jesus prepared his disciples for that awful absence his death would bring. He knew their grief; he knew it could destroy them. He promised to send them his Spirit, the Spirit of Truth, or "the Advocate" (John 14:16, 26; 15:26; 16:7). When the Greek word for "Advocate," *parakletos,* is translated as "the Comforter," as some biblical translations have it, we see the resonance between the sending of the Spirit and the blessing of this beatitude, in which another form of the word is used, *paraklethesontai* "to promise comfort."

While mourners may choose consolation over advocacy in the immediate aftermath of loss, over time they will need both. We need people to stand *with* us in our pain; we also need people to stand *for* us when we are too tired to stand up for ourselves. I remember the wail of a freshly minted widow: "I could barely get out of bed in the morning. How was I going to get death certificates to everyone who wanted one?" A faithful son-in-law stepped in and did the work for her. He stood *with* her in her grief; he stood *for* her as they sorted through the mountain of paperwork that erupted in the wake of a death. As you can see, biblical understandings of advocacy and comfort are closely linked together. As we look again at Simeon's prophecy in Luke 2:25, the Greek words show new urgency: he longed for "the consolation of Israel," *paraklesin tou Israel.* That hope is both spiritual and political. Jesus promises a comfort of both kinds.

Divine Blessings Abound

Abraham's wife, Sarah, wanted to hoard her blessings, ensuring that her offspring, not Hagar's, would be the seed of a great nation. She feared there were not enough blessings to go around: if Ishmael got any, Isaac would have that many fewer for himself. The same thing happened with the Israelites in the wilderness. They worried the supply of manna would become exhausted, and so they tried to hoard more than their daily portion. When they took more than they needed, it spoiled (Exodus 16). Neither Sarah nor the Israelites trusted in the abundance of divine blessing. Divine blessing is not a zero-sum game; divine blessing is the gift that keeps on giving. There is always more than you need.

The country of mourning breeds a reckless and holy confidence. It is a spirit of "what-the-hellness," as a friend once put it. With that said, he broke into a bad rendition of one of Janis Joplin's greatest hits: "When you ain't got nothin', you got nothin' to lose." He could not hold a tune, but his words held a lot of truth. Loss is strangely liberating, untethering people from familiar moorings and leaving them open to anything. If they cannot find any bearings, people drift into despair. But some people often find that loss anchors them deeper in a mystery that holds them. The apostle Paul names this mystery in his letter to the Romans:

> [W]e also boast in our sufferings, knowing that suffering produces endurance, and endurance produces character, and character produces hope, and hope does not disappoint us, because God's love has been poured into our hearts through the Holy Spirit that has been given to us. (Romans 5:3-5)

This is a tough recipe for building character, but Paul promises that the black hole of absence will not remain empty forever. Love fills in the cracks of longing. Moreover, love comes from the very one whom disciples mourn. Only Christ can offer the comfort they crave. The love of the Risen Christ comes in unexpected ways, some dazzling and others so ordinary we do not even notice them. But love pours down like manna in the wilderness of Sinai. Like the ancient Israelites, all we need to do is pick up what we need for the day.

When my husband was dying, we found manna aplenty, and it sustained us. We refused to live without joy, taking refuge, instead, in what I came to call "the daily graces." As we wandered in the wilderness, we discovered that a table had been prepared for us. Daily manna fell for us, often in unexpected ways. We tried out a new recipe, and it worked. We plotted a new route for the daily walk, and it was beautiful. Friends brought an entire Thanksgiving dinner to our doorstep—in July. At night, we counted our blessings; there were many. On the worst days, we laughed, saying that "the best thing that happened today was that it ended." Those days were actually few in number; we were being tutored in the daily graces. God's love was poured into our hearts.

Remembering the Dead and Being Remembered

On the Festival of All Saints (November 1), Christians pause to remember their foremothers and forefathers in the faith. The texts for that day always include the beatitudes from Matthew's Gospel. This is no coincidence. As we pause to remember the saints, we discover to our great surprise that they were doing this first. They have been busy remembering us, and not just in the sense of thinking about us and calling us to the mind of God. The saints remember us in a real way, fashioning us anew bone on bone, sinew on sinew. Now we are ready to tackle the chapter's opening question: how do the saints spend their days? And that answer is threefold: they bless, comfort, and re-member us.

If the Revelation of John climaxes the entire sweep of Scripture, then we get some great snapshots into the daily schedule of the saints. They abandon themselves to blessing.

> Blessing and glory and wisdom
> and thanksgiving and honor
> and power and might
> be to our God forever and ever! (Revelation 7:12)

Praise flows effortlessly from the lips of the saints because they are unbound, liberated from e-mail, iPods™, and Blackberries™, from deadlines and committee meetings, and from papers and exams. Martin Luther captures this liberation when he describes Adam in the Garden of Eden. He writes of Adam before the incident with the fruit, before the Fall and the first dress code, as Adam was oblivious that he was naked or mortal and was unaware of the knowledge of good and evil, as well as the difference between them. This was Adam as God intended him. Luther imagines him "intoxicated with rejoicing toward God and . . . delighted with all the other creatures."[4] Call him "drunk on God" if you wish: that is what Adam was up to in the garden. The soundtrack for Luther's description should be that great chorus from Handel's *Messiah*: "Blessing and honor, glory and power, be unto Him." Restored to their created goodness, the saints spend their days drunk on God. Let the people say "Rock on!"

We rock with the saints. When we gather to worship and when we assemble to praise, the veil between the worlds of the living and the dead is lifted. If only for a moment, we worship with the communion of saints. The architects of medieval cathedrals understood this, as they built this conviction into their churches. They designed the space so that the nave was big enough to accommodate the crowd of the living. The priest stood at an altar in the chancel, his back to the people. Nobody worried that they were looking at the back of the priest— partly because the view of his vestments from the rear was so beautiful. But it was not really about vestments anyway. It was about worshipping in the communion of saints, for the priest and the people filled only half of a circle of blessing. In front of them, completing the circle, were the saints. They lay in tombs underneath the altar or in the crypt behind it; they loomed above the altar in vibrant stained glass windows. The saints were everywhere, and they completed the circle. As the worship continued, the living joined the dead in a song of ceaseless praise.

Questions for Reflection

1. Has loss opened new possibilities in your own life? How? Who are some of the saints you remember frequently? Why do you call them "saints"? What blessings do they continue to bring to you? How do people who are still alive bless you—even unexpectedly?

2. What other blessings do you find in the story of Hagar and Ishmael? Are there other Old Testament guides for the country of mourning?: Ruth mourning the loss of her husband (Ruth 1); David torn between his love for Jonathan and the enmity of Saul (1 Samuel 20-31); Jephthah's daughter mourning her virginity (Judges 11:29-40). What blessings have you found from your own wilderness of grief?

3. What other blessings do you find in the story of Mary's mourning? Are there other New Testament guides for the country of mourning? the lament of mothers who lost their children in Herod's slaughter of the innocents (Matthew 2:16-18); the sharp grief of Mary and

Martha at the death of their brother Lazarus (John 11:1-44); Judas'
shock over his own betrayal of Jesus (Matthew 27:3-5); Peter's grief
over his betrayal of Jesus (Matthew 26:69-75; Mark 14:66-72; Luke
22:54-62; John 18:15-27)? How has blessing found you?

For Further Reflection

Psalm 30

This psalm does not begin with thanksgiving: it leads with lament.
The psalmist begins in Sheol, the home of the dead. But we join the
psalmist's journey into light; we follow him into rejoicing. With him,
we are invited to sing: "Weeping may linger for the night, but joy comes
with the morning" (v. 5). With him, we are invited to hope for that turn
from "mourning into dancing" (v. 11).

4

Following with Tempered Strength

Blessed are the meek, for they will inherit the earth.

—Matthew 5:5

The motto of the Dependent Organization of Really Meek and Timid Souls (DOORMATS) is "The meek shall inherit the earth—if there are no objections." It's an appropriate choice given conventional wisdom that "Meek means weak." Divine logic, however, begs to differ.

Two biblical portraits, those of Moses and Jesus, edit the "wimp factor" out of popular misconceptions of meekness, showing these understandings to be "meekness-lite." Biblical meekness is tempered strength, power deliberately held in check. It becomes a disposition important for disciples. It is at the heart of Jesus' invitation to all disciples when he asks those who are weary and heavy with burdens to take his yoke, his burden, upon them so that he can give them rest. Central to biblical meekness is the ability to attend to God. The practice of holy conversation invites us to humble ourselves before the Word of God, finding in it rest from whatever burdens us.

Tempered Power in an Intemperate World

Watching Uncle Irving get mad was like watching a volcano erupt in slow motion. It started in the hands, which clenched into tight little fists. Then red spread up the neck, around each ear, onto the face, and finally words poured from the mouth. The words were not nasty; there were just a lot of them. To a child of eight, the overall effect was impressive. Once I asked my father about his brother. "Well," he said, a smile playing on his lips, "Irving has always had a short fuse." My father, in contrast, had a long fuse. He was even and steady, a man who planted terrariums in great green hand-blown glass bottles while waiting for spring. He had a center of gravity that grounded us all.

Meekness marked the difference between the two men, one short-tempered and the other long-tempered. That difference points toward the violent gap between power held in check and power running amok. My uncle's explosions show the real enemy of meekness to be unchecked impulse. He wanted *what* he wanted *when* he wanted it. Frustrated by his own predicament, he simply blew up. Impulse unleashes anger whenever things do not go our way.

The meek person is not dictated as much by outcomes and is more protected from squalls of rage, circumstance, or misfortune. She weathers storms because she has a deep anchor. Often that commitment is unilateral. My father frequently got caught in the wake of his brother's rage. It would have been both easy and tempting to reciprocate these rants. Instead, he put up with the attacks of anger, refusing to retaliate in kind. An even keel contained the conflict and kept it from escalating.

If we project this domestic drama onto an international screen, we see a desperate need for tempered power. While logic of revenge dictates an eye for an eye and a tooth for a tooth, political meekness counsels peace, unilaterally if necessary. Only meekness is strong enough to stop the cycle of violence that pits Israeli against Palestinian, Sunni against Shiite, and Christian against Muslim.

Of course, the danger is that if you don't get your licks in, you'll get licked. Biblical meekness, however, moves beyond a human calculus of winners and losers to rest in a divine order. In patience, the meek wait for God's will to break in. Being patient is a lot like being *a patient*. A friend who logged long hours in the hospital undergoing treatment observed that being a patient was a lot different than being an agent. He was used to taking charge and being in control, in short, being an agent. In the hospital, though, "I am always having things done to me; I can't do much for myself."

But there the difference between biblical meekness and being a patient ends. Being a patient breeds passivity; meekness never does. With quiet defiance, my friend chose not to be defined by his disease.

He refused to live by medical truths, powerful though they were. Instead, he took his compass from spiritual truths. He ceded his own agency to God: "The doctors love me," he joked. "All I want them to be is good docs. I don't expect them to be God. That job is already taken." The God who held my friend holds all of us. Biblical meekness has an infinite fuse, stretching to eternity and anchored firmly in the heart of God. The psalmist reads out God's EKG: God is "slow to anger and abounding in steadfast love" (Psalm 103:8).

As we survey the carnage that wars leave behind, we are humbled and relieved to know that God does not respond in kind. God not only is long-suffering, but God also became one of us to share our suffering and show us the pathways of peace. Through Jesus, we know the meekness of a God who suffers with us, enveloping us in a Father's love.

Moses: Mighty and Meek

The Hebrew scriptures present Moses as meekness personified: "Now the man Moses was very meek, above all the men which were upon the face of the earth" (Numbers 12:3, KJV).

Yet, the meekest man on the face of the earth needs no fewer than four books of the Bible for his story. The Moses story begins in the bulrushes of Exodus 2 and ends with him buried in an unknown grave at the end of the book of Deuteronomy, not in the promised land but in view of it. Because much of the material embraced in Moses' biography recites the laws governing the Hebrew people, it is easy to miss the story threading through the legal code. When we tease out the narrative, however, we meet a man of considerable backbone who wasn't afraid to object when he felt objection was warranted. Moses was no wimp; he could growl when he needed to. He embodied the biblical disposition of meekness: tempered strength and power held in check. Moses would be thrown out of DOORMATS in an instant, that is if the group could ever bring itself to protest.

Moses' adult life began with a murder, as he witnessed an Egyptian beating one of his kinsfolk. Moses responded with untempered power: he killed the Egyptian and went into hiding (Exodus 2:11-15). This was a man capable of rage.

Moses objected mightily when God called him from a burning bush to lead the Israelites out of the land of Egypt. Before we read his protest as mere whining, it is worth remembering that he was looking into an inferno—barefoot! Still, he objected, not once, but four times: he questioned his own credentials; he questioned God's; he argued that a speech impediment compromised his leadership; and he suggested God choose someone else (Exodus 3:1—4:17). God remained undaunted. Perhaps impressed with Moses' ability to stand up for himself, God thought even better of choosing him to lead the people out of slavery in Egypt.

At times, we see Moses' temper flare spectacularly during the course of his leadership. In an incident at Meribah, Moses acted out of character. Fed up with the Israelites' constant complaints that he had led them into the desert where they would die for lack of water and food, Moses made bringing water from a rock at Meribah look like a magic trick that he and Aaron performed rather than the mighty act of God that it was (Numbers 20:9-13). This time he paid dearly for his anger. After leading the people through the wilderness to the promised land, God barred Moses from entering it. He died on Mount Nebo in full view of an inheritance he would not enjoy. Moses' anger also flared against the Israelites when, upon his descent from Mt. Sinai, he discovered that they had built a golden calf to worship during his absence. In anger Moses threw the tablets down, breaking them, and then burned the golden calf (Exodus 32:19-20).

Moses even got angry with God. He registered shock that God would allow his chosen people to suffer at the hands of the Egyptians (Exodus 5:22). Then after the people were set free and began worshipping the golden calf, Moses met God's wrath against the faithless people with a wrath of his own: "O Lord, why does your wrath burn hot against your people, whom you brought out of the land of Egypt with great power and with a mighty hand?" (Exodus 32:11) Moses did not protect anyone from his anger, not even the living God. Moses' ability to stand up for himself and his people seems only to have endeared him to God: it built up that relationship rather than destroying it.

Yet, there is ample biblical evidence for a meek-mannered Moses. He held his power in check when he needed to. He endured the disdain of Pharaoh, who, as Moses predicted, found this stammering youth a ludicrous leader. He suffered Aaron's spinelessness as a leader (Exodus 32:21-24), and his spitefulness (along with Miriam's) in regard to his foreign-born wife (Numbers 12:1-16). He put up with the people's murmuring in the desert as they complained about bread one moment and meat the next. He even endured God's anger with his actions at Meribah (Numbers 20:12; Deuteronomy 32:50-52). Moses humbly accepted God's judgment that he would never cross into the promised land. The children of the faithless people would inherit the land—but not the man who had faithfully led them.

What is going on here? Biblical meekness seems to be volatile, bold at its best and grossly unfair at its worst. How did Moses know when to stand up for what he needed and to stand back when he had to? The golden calf incident unlocks biblical meekness. It could have isolated Moses from his people on one hand and from his God on the other. A lesser leader would have simply thrown up his hands in despair and hiked into the desert where he could at least die in peace. Yet, Moses never walked away from either his God or his people. Pleading before the people for God's will and pleading before God for the people's lives, he stayed with God's wilderness program. He shows us that tenacity is at the heart of biblical meekness.

You have got to admire a leader like that—and God clearly did. The flare-up over the golden calf only bound God and Moses more deeply together. Only after that incident did Moses receive a visit from God himself. God spoke with him "face to face, as one speaks to a friend" (Exodus 33:11), and God granted him a revelation of divine goodness, passing by him in full divine glory. What did Moses see?

The Lord, the Lord, a God merciful and gracious, slow to anger, and abounding in steadfast love and faithfulness. (Exodus 34:6)

Moses saw into the heart of God. He found there an infinitely long temper and awesome power held in check for the sake of a beloved people. God is meekness itself.

Moses died in full view of a land he would not inherit. Yet, the last words out of his mouth were words of blessing, not regret. Moses' blessings fell on everyone, not just the few in the pack who had not caused any trouble. As he breathed his last, Moses rained blessings upon his troubled people. Not surprisingly, they streamed down like manna in a desert (Deuteronomy 33).

Jesus: Meek and Humble of Heart

Neither was Moses' New Testament counterpart a doormat. Jesus may have entered Jerusalem the week of his death "meek, and sitting upon an ass" (Matthew 21:5, KJV),[1] but he caused quite a ruckus during his lifetime. He objected to money changers in his Father's house and drove them out with a fury that was not at all meek. He shook off social convention, reaching out to street kids and Samaritan women. He ate and drank with people whom no one considered respectable tablemates.

Jesus perfected Moses' meekness. His power was indisputable. Jesus cast out demons, healed lepers, restored sight to the blind, and spoke "with authority" (Mark 1:27). He walked on water, calmed stormy seas, and fed hungry masses with a boy's meal. Like Moses, he objected to divine intent—only to set his face toward Jerusalem in obedience to God's will.

We think we know the story of Jesus by heart. Yet, reading it through Moses' eyes offers a new perspective on a familiar narrative. Certainly, there are the surface similarities between each man's might and meekness. The same man who worked miracles and cleansed temples would not lift a finger to save himself. He submitted without protest to his crucifixion, just as Moses accepted God's judgment that he would not enter the promised land. Indeed, as the Passion grinds to its horrific conclusion, Jesus becomes more and more mute, letting the psalms tell a story for which he cannot find words.

But there are deeper similarities. Moses met a God who identified himself only as "I AM." John's Gospel gives the details of this identity. Jesus speaks the same words in this Gospel that God does from the burning bush, but he finishes the sentence: "I am the bread of life" (6:35); I am the "living water" (7:37-38); "I am the light of the world" (8:12);

"I am the good shepherd" (10:11); "I am the resurrection and the life" (11:25); "I am the way, and the truth, and the life" (14:6); "I am the true vine" (15:1). Suddenly, a God clouded in mystery manifests in ordinary images of bread, water and vine, and shepherds and lamps. Jesus reveals the meekness of God: power held in check so that believers might eat and drink, see and be safe.

There are two times when, like Moses, Jesus speaks with God face-to-face. The first is the Transfiguration (Matthew 17:1-8; Mark 9:2-8; Luke 9:28-36). Should we be surprised that the Gospels record Moses as being there? He too has seen God passing by, and now he emerges to support another friend of God, God's son. Like Moses' face as he descended the mountain after receiving the second set of tablets from God (Exodus 34:29-30), Jesus' face shone like the sun. Jesus encounters God again in Gethsemane, and this time the conversation is not so easy. Like Moses objected to his appointment as leader of the Israelites, Jesus protests his commissioning: "Abba, Father, for you all things are possible; remove this cup from me." Then, he retracts his power and falls into the divine embrace, saying "yet, not what I want, but what you want" (Mark 14:36).

The Spirit's meekness is unwittingly attested to by those who mocked Jesus on the cross saying, "He saved others; he cannot save himself" (Matthew 27:42). But a soldier attending his crucifixion knows the truth: "Truly this man was God's son." (Matthew 27:54). It is the meek who will inherit the earth—not the occupying army.

Perhaps the soldiers glimpse for an instant where the intense energies of war will lead them. Power unchecked leaves only carnage in its wake. Perhaps the meek inherit the earth because they are the only ones left standing. But there is a deeper message here. No one can measure up to divine meekness: there is too much war in our world and, worse, war in our souls. If Moses, the Old Testament icon of meekness, could not make it into the promised land, what hope is there for us? We cannot measure up to Moses—even when he is angry.

The good news is that we do not need to. Jesus, too, died with a blessing: "Father, forgive them; for they do not know what they are doing" (Luke 23:34). Jesus demonstrates meekness more fully than Moses does.

He does not turn his back on anyone, not even those who persecute him. We stand in that crowd, whether we would play the part of the fainthearted disciples, the faithful and fearless women, or the brutalizing Roman soldiers. Whatever part we play, we are forgiven. Like Moses' final benediction, Jesus' last blessing falls on a troubled world like manna from heaven. This food not only sustains us, but also gives us life.

And just in case the disciples did not get the message because they were clueless or, more likely, had fled the scene to avoid capture themselves, Jesus returns to make the same point. John's Gospel has no Last Supper, not even the words of institution. Instead, Jesus' final meal comes with a foot washing, the ultimate gesture of meekness (John 13:1-11). Then, John includes a "first breakfast," as Jesus returns after the resurrection to feed his disciples breakfast (John 21:1-23). He does not order out or miraculously produce a gourmet brunch. Rather, in a characteristic gesture of humility, the Lord of the Universe prepares the meal himself. Jesus is divine power poured out in service. Order up!

An Invitation to Inherit the Earth

The One who incarnates meekness issues an invitation to all disciples: "Come to me, all you that are weary and are carrying heavy burdens, and I will give you rest. Take my yoke upon you, and learn from me; for I am gentle (*praus*) and humble in heart, and you will find rest for your souls. For my yoke is easy, and my burden is light" (Matthew 11:28-30). After examining the two portraits of the Bible's meekest, we should all be rushing to take up the yoke Jesus offers. We rush to follow for three reasons.

First, we know that he speaks the truth about his own meekness. But we also know the qualities that make for biblical meekness. We know the strength that is its foundation. Both these men knew how to flash their wrath, particularly in the face of injustice. You would want someone like that watching your back, and you would hate to be confronted with such anger. Moreover, that anger made exception for no one—not even God himself—when the stakes were high. Finally, we know the tenacity meekness indicates. Neither Jesus nor Moses ever walked away, not even from those who persecuted them.

The anger of Moses and Jesus never destroyed a relationship but somehow only served to make it stronger. God received Moses' rage as a gift: it only garnered Moses greater favor. From the cross, Jesus cannot find it in his heart to be angry with the people who killed him. It is clear Jesus cannot forgive them on his own, for he never says "I forgive you." Perhaps Jesus senses that any parent would be bent on avenging the death of a child, his own Father included. And Jesus makes the gesture that addresses both problems. He knows forgiveness is the only way forward. When he cannot find it in his own heart, he binds his Father to forgiveness, not retaliation. It is the only way for any of us to find rest.

Second, think about all the yokes you bear. I know I bear many. "The List" wakes me each morning: things to do, deadlines to meet, calls to make, people to see. All my burdens kick me into waking, each demanding a particular attention. By the time I get to the coffeepot, I am exhausted. I sag with the day's demands, and I have not even had that first cup.

Think of the yokes you bear, such as the yoke of children and parents, the yoke of caring for a household, the yoke of vocation, and the yokes of friendship, citizenship, and profession. We bear a lot of burdens! And our shoulders ache with the weight. By inviting us to "take my yoke upon you," Jesus invites us to acknowledge all the burdens and then asks us to consider whether his yoke would be lighter.

I remember my mother trying to manage a household composed of a busy husband, two small children as different as night and day, and an aging mother-in-law. We were stuffed into one of Baltimore's tiny brick row houses. We all had our own demands, and most of them were directed to her. Her yokes were many, none of them easy. The yoke Jesus offered would have been light in comparison. I also know that his yoke for her was caring for all of us in her own wonderfully wacky way. If she only could have seen more clearly that Jesus was there with her, bearing her up with power and tenacity. Jesus invites us to take up his yoke and promises to bear it with us.

Third, Jesus promises what we need most in a world of burdens: rest. It is a commodity in short supply; no one ever has enough. Moses and Jesus found it only by dying, though I wonder how much of Moses' time covenanting with the Lord on Mount Sinai for forty days and forty nights was spent sleeping. I hope he got a good chance to catch up on sleep that was lost while he was trying to shepherd the lost sheep of the house of Israel. He did not even get to rest in the promised land. God's judgment seems unfair until we read it against the backdrop of this beatitude: "Blessed are the meek, for they will inherit the earth."

Jesus uttered this blessing with Moses in mind, restoring to him the land he never got to enter. In this blessing, Moses finally makes it to the promised land. Jesus' gift to Moses is also ours. All we have to do is say yes.

Meekness in Speech: Holy Conversations

This is a time in both the churches and the public square when words become weapons. Slurs and slogans hog tie civil discourse in all kinds of settings. When all sides claim divine justification, we find it hard to remember our common humanity as children of a loving God. We could use a little more verbal meekness. Moses and Jesus give disciples some ground rules for holy conversation.

1. Start a difficult conversation with a prayer pause and take as many as you need during the course of the conversation. Parents usually call for time outs at the end of an argument or behavioral malfunction, but what if time outs also came at the beginning? I know a busy executive who takes a time out whenever he knows a tough call is coming in. He lets the phone ring three times before answering. The pause centers him. Another CEO pauses before a window as she heads into a difficult meeting. As she looks out onto the well-tended corporate grounds, she summons up what is really important to her: her family, her faith, her friends, and the beauty surrounding her. At our faculty meetings, we sound a gong every hour for thirty seconds of silence, whatever the topic is and however heated the discussion becomes. It cools things down if they need cooling, gives us rest if we need resting, and allows us to refocus. After the golden calf incident, Moses lingered with God, letting his wrath cool. Even Jesus escaped

the needy crowds to go up into the mountains to pray. Conversations that begin with prayer, vocalized or not, go more smoothly.

2. Try taking the other side; see things from the other point of view. Meekness means climbing out of your own self-interest to see the interests of others. True humility allows us to step out of the cesspool of self-delusion. Often people caught in the crossfire develop this skill as a survival tool. Moses became good at representing God's side to the people and the people's side to God. He was effective only because he imagined himself in their sandals. We are not going to reach Moses' level of diplomatic expertise, but he reminds us of an important truth. When we can imagine where the other person is coming from, only then are we ready to talk. As we gain experience at this particular skill of holy conversation, we ready ourselves to obey Jesus' impossible command to love the enemy and pray for our persecutors (Matthew 5:44).

3. Cultivate tenacity. Sometimes it is hard to stay with a difficult conversation or a hard situation. Most of us talk things through only to a point. Whether there is a pressing deadline or a desire to flee, something else intervenes, and holy conversation short-circuits. Meekness commits to the long haul, a commitment that can be expressed creatively and forcefully. You may need to be clear how much time you have for conversation so that no one feels slighted by the clock. In congregational settings where volatile issues are scheduled for discussion, it is crucial to set a time frame and stick to it. Always the last question should be "Do we need to come back to this?"

It is also true that some things can be over-talked, covering the same ground over and over again with little forward motion. As one of my nephews lamented a high school crush: "All she wants to do is *talk* about the relationship. I just want to *have* it!" People may have different needs for conversation, and the same holds true for groups. They certainly have different styles of conversing.

The secret to holding holy conversation is assuring people that whatever happens, you will be there for each other. Nothing said can break that core commitment to be there. Remember Moses' tenacity with God and Jesus' with his disciples.

4. Use "I" language. The "I AM" statements from John's Gospel recall Moses and the burning bush. That fiery encounter shows us that both God and Moses know who they are. God drops a calling card, "I AM WHO I AM," but Moses also knows who he is. For someone who has been interrupted while doing something else, he shows remarkable presence. He knows where his blind spots are, as well as those of his people. He has identified all the potential pitfalls. He anticipates where he will need help, and he asks for it. Using "I" language can keep arguments from going cosmic. Knowing who you are, where you need help, and asking for it are all good pointers for holy conversation.

5. Use anger to build up, not to destroy. A few unconsidered words can easily destroy a relationship built up over a lifetime. A lot of people hold in their discontent because of its devastatingly destructive potential. Those who do hold it in find that it eats them away on the inside or erupts in even less appropriate circumstances.

Holy conversation does not mean pulling your punches. Meekness does not erase the power of anger, but it holds it in check. Before expressing frustration, think of whether it can be heard and how it might be received. I've discovered that travel is frequently an opportunity for frustration. As I hung out in Paris with another family, I knew something would blow up. I just did not know how we would handle it. When the crash came, we talked it out, prefacing it with memories of all the good times we had had and all the improbable things that had gone right.

Sometimes people need the gift of your anger, but only if it serves to build up. Anger can enhance a relationship when people know nothing will shake the foundation off its base. Following the travel incident in Paris, my friend and I sat at a café and talked about what had happened. "I knew there would be a crash," I ventured. She raised her glass to me and smiled, saying, "I knew we'd get through it." That confidence had a lot of love behind it. I felt the same way. We moved forward from that point.

Biblical meekness does not hold back anger, particularly in the face of injustice. Perhaps the world's leaders fear that the meek will inherit the earth, which is why they cling all the more violently to their need for control. I once watched the fathers of two dead boys, one Israeli and the other Palestinian, speak out jointly for peace in the Middle East. I know Jesus' promise is true: I am putting my money on the meek.

Questions for Reflection

1. What issues make you "see red?" How do you decide when to stand up and when to stand back? What happens when communities, congregations, or nations "see red?"

2. Have you ever tempered your power? Were you glad? What happened?

3. Moses was mighty, meek, and, finally, a friend of God. What would it be like to have such a relationship with God?

4. Moses loved his people, but they were often hard to like and, at times, exasperating. What is it like to be bound to such a family or community? Jesus, too, loved his disciples deeply, but at times their ignorance irritated him. When Jesus and Moses finally met at the Transfiguration, what advice to you think Moses gave Jesus?

For Further Reflection

Psalm 37

This psalm includes the promise, "the meek shall inherit the earth" and adds great counsel for those who would practice meekness, warning disciples of the corrosive vices of envy, jealousy, anxiety, and anger. "Be still before the Lord, and wait patiently for him," the psalmist advises. Stillness requires emptying ourselves. And as we clear the desk of all that troubles us, we realize God has been sitting there quietly, waiting for us all along.

5

Follow Your Heart and Find the Heart of God

Blessed are those who hunger and thirst for righteousness, for they will be filled.

—Matthew 5:6

"Follow your heart," people often advise. This counsel makes sense, considering all the other body parts that lead us around: the myopic eyes, lifeless reason, untethered impulse, the mysterious nose, or some other piece of the human anatomy. But the advice proves even wiser on a different level. Consider how often we follow not our own heart, but someone else's, by living up—or down!—to that person's desires and expectations for us. A young woman confided, "I was living out my mother's dreams." Once she got a handle on her own dreams, she steered her life into smoother waters.

There is one heart we should pay attention to, and that is the heart of God. We attend to God's heart, not out of duty or responsibility, but because of a deep homing instinct. God made us; we bear the divine trademark. To get our hands on the operating manual for the human heart, we only need only to find the heart of God. There lies the most reliable guide to the human heart.

This means that God's deepest desires for us resonate with our own. The fourth-century African Christian Saint Augustine (354–430) put the matter memorably: "Our heart is restless until it rests in you." He also explains the heart's restlessness: "You have made us for yourself."[1] Augustine knew what he was talking about. He followed other people's hearts around for much of his youth, loving recklessly and without satisfaction. Augustine's longing was never filled. What satisfies the human heart? This beatitude answers boldly and without equivocation: the righteousness of God.

As we probe this beatitude, we find a rough guide to the human heart, focusing on the disposition of love. Not surprisingly, we find that path leads straight into the heart of God. As we hunger and thirst for what God hungers and thirsts for, we entwine our heartstrings with God's. What does God want from us? From command to love song to hymn, everything in Scripture comes to the same conclusion: God wants nothing more and nothing less than love. Indeed, "God so loved the world that he gave his only Son" (John 3:16).

A child is the love of its parents, passion expressed in flesh and blood. In the same way, Jesus is God's passion for us. Jesus tutors disciples in the passion of God, so that they might love as God loves, holding in their hearts those who are dear to God's heart. Disciples express this love in the practice of love that extends even to the enemy.

Searching Hearts Both Human and Divine

A locker room buddy lamented aloud that her teenage daughter was aggressively trying to be unlovable. "I love her so much it hurts," Suzanne said. She blamed herself for not loving well enough, steadily enough, or expressively enough. The way she saw it, she had failed at love. We all know the feeling and the realities that feed it. There are the grand failures. Couples break up after pledging "until death do us part." Parents and children divorce each other in judgmental silences. Wars erupt over boundaries, religious division, and ethnic tension. Poverty and prejudice and hunger testify mutely to extraordinary failures of loving. Then there are the ordinary failings: a harsh word, a rumor whispered into a waiting ear, and a shred of gossip woven into the false story. How do we fail at love? Let me count the ways!

With deadly accuracy, the prophet Jeremiah read the EKG of the human heart: "More tortuous than all else is the human heart, beyond remedy; who can understand it?" (Jeremiah 17:9-10, New American Bible [NAB])[2] We fail at love, in great ways and in small ones, yet love exists as a miracle of grace in our midst. Twelfth-century Cistercian mystic Bernard of Clairvaux (1090–1153) chronicled love and its failings. Yet, he paid equal attention to the traces of grace along the way. In a remarkable reflection he called "On Loving God," Bernard began by presenting love as the bottom-feeder it so often is, a thinly veiled excuse for self-interest: "I love you—because of what you can do for me." We have all experienced pure utility disguised as love. Yet, Bernard found something in the embers of such opportunism. Gradually, grace redirects desire, and the lover says, "I love you because you're good to me." As the breath of grace keeps blowing, love burns brighter: "I love you because you're good." Finally, the embers catch fire: "I love you because you're you." Bernard speaks of loving God; he could just as easily have been speaking of human love.[3] So often love begins in narcissism: the heart turns in on itself. But over time grace straightens our tightly coiled affection so that it reaches beyond the self to another and then through the other to God, the source and spirit of all loving. For Bernard, wherever we find it and however flawed it may be in its initial manifestation, human love whispers of the divine. Our attempts at loving are a foretaste of the divine embrace to come.

Maybe if Martin Luther had been French like Bernard instead of being German, he would have worried more about love than trust. Instead, Luther fretted about finding a gracious God—and then trusting that gracious God to actually be gracious. The words he clung to as a young and tortured monk tell it all. He did not plead "I am yours; love me!" But "I am yours; save me!"

Yet, Luther loved Bernard. He discovered in the monk a reforming spirit like his own; he even caught Bernard's passion. Once Luther found that gracious God, he turned to love, both our love for God and God's love for us. Like Jeremiah, he knew the "tortuous" ways of the human heart. In his explanation of the first commandment, Luther wisely observed: "That to which your heart clings and entrusts itself is, I say, really your God."[4] He was less optimistic than Bernard about our ability to love God. He put his money on God's love for us.[5] As human love ascends Bernard's ladder, climbing toward a holy love in mystical union, Luther shows God's love coming down, descending into our feeble and fickle human hearts. He captured that movement in his Christmas hymn: "All praise to you, eternal Lord, clothed in garb of flesh and blood, a manger choosing for a throne while worlds on worlds are yours alone. Hallelujah!"[6] As we trace Jesus' life from that Christmas manger to his death and resurrection beyond, Suzanne's locker room lament rings true in a very different way. God loves us so much that it hurts. Beyond the manger is the Crucifixion, the extent to which God would go to assure us of his love. But, beyond the Crucifixion is the Resurrection, a promise that God's love will conquer all.

God loves us through the love of others, and when we love, however imperfectly, we spread that joy. We are God's hands in a world that longs for the divine embrace. We may fail at love, but God's love never fails us.

The Steadfast and Passionate Divine Heart

At a nationally televised football game, someone seems to have a permanent seat at the fifty-yard line, and that someone always bears the same sign: "John 3:16." Anyone who has been to Sunday school knows the verse: "For God so loved the world that he gave his only Son. . . ." That verse in the context of network television and professional sports sheds new light on a familiar passage. Football is a game of calculation: yards rushed, points scored, minutes remaining in each quarter. If you are told in that context that "God so loved the world," you want to know exactly how much. You pose the religious equivalent of the poet's question: "How do I love thee? Let me count the ways."[7]

We get some of love's arithmetic in the Bible—and in unexpected places. Language of love softens the Decalogue, and a passage familiar for its demands suddenly sounds like a lover's pleading. "Don't you remember me? Don't you remember everything that happened to us? Think of all I did for you: I led you out of the land of Egypt, out of the house of bondage. What more do you want? Can't you love me the way I love you?" The first commandment seems to portray a jealous and punitive God—until you do the math. In fact, the commandment promises that God's love far surpasses God's anger. God's anger only lasts for three or four generations, but God's love extends for a thousand. Do the math: "For I the Lord your God am a jealous God, punishing children for the iniquity of parents, to the third and the fourth generation of those who reject me, but showing steadfast love to the thousandth generation of those who love me and keep my command-ments" (Exodus 20:5-6).

Wouldn't it be great if human love were as lasting and human anger so brief. As I speak with children of abusive parents, I discover that the parents who abused them had themselves been beaten. Behind them were more abusing parents who had been abused by parents who had themselves been abused. I uncover a chain of domestic violence extend-ing back generation upon generation. In comparison, God's anger seems short-lived. Furthermore, God returns love with love, and not on a *quid pro quo* basis, but with an abundance that spills down the centuries.

The Song of Solomon makes divine longing even more explicit, and Scripture's greatest love song pulses with erotic energy. Voices of a male lover and a female lover wind around each other like lovers' bodies—it is no wonder that the word *intercourse* can be used both for both conversa-tion and also sexual congress. God's longing for us is passionate, focused, and intense. Perhaps the woman's dream sequence puts it best with its intended repetition of "him whom my soul loves" (Song of Solomon 3:1-4). God longs for us the way two lovers long for each other.

That longing does not diminish when we break faith. The prophet Hosea describes the faithfulness of a man who marries a woman unable to be faithful to him. Gomer bears three children, none of whom seem to be Hosea's. Yet, he faithfully searches her out, brings her back under his roof, and receives her as his wife (Hosea 1, 3). The Hosea/Gomer relationship stands for the God/Israel relationship. We may protest that experience shows women to be more faithful than men, and we may object to gender stereotyping; but when played on a divine-human stage, the parable of Hosea and Gomer stings because of its truth. How have I failed to love God? Let me count the ways!

In such moments of truth, it is good to know that God's heart is jealous. No matter how many other lovers we yearn for, God welcomes us back with open arms. The parable of the prodigal son is finally the parable of the gracious father (Luke 15:11-32). From wherever we have strayed, God welcomes us home: "Let us eat and celebrate; for this son of mine was dead and is alive again; he was lost and is found!"

Hosea and the Song of Solomon are almost embarrassingly sexual. They depict God's love as deeply passionate, charged with an *eros* that rattles us polite, private Lutherans. We prefer to think of God's love more abstractly. It is like sunshine that falls without passion or discrimination on street and silo, on rich and poor alike. The sun does not need to know where it falls in order to bring about light. Passionate love, on the contrary, knows the lover's body and soul like the palm of the hand. Every gesture registers; every glance delights.

Maybe we should reconsider our generalized, antiseptic approach to God's love, embracing instead the charged erotic rhetoric of these biblical authors. God loves us not in the abstract but in the specific, even and especially our flaws. Read through the first chapters of the Song of Solomon and notice how concrete the lover is about the beloved. You can almost see the skin of the beloved; you can almost touch it. Love is in the details.

After her husband died, a widow found a journal he had left behind. An entry he wrote listed, in detail, everything about her that delighted him: "converses easily with strangers; finds energy to do things and yet is willing to rest; is able to sit in silence for prayer; makes humor of a tight situation; likes to anticipate and plan the events of our excellent adventure. . . ." His love for her had been so specific. Then she remembered his ready response to a friend who had asked this long-time bachelor how he liked being married. "I like being married to *her!*" he said. "You don't marry an institution; you marry a person."

God is like that with each of us. God does not love *humanity* in general or even the world in the abstract. God loves each of us with the kind of detail the woman found in her husband's journal. Take the psalmist's words seriously:

O Lord, you have searched me and known me.
    You know when I sit down and when I rise up;
        you discern my thoughts from far away.
    You search out my path and my lying down,
        and are acquainted with all my ways. (Psalm 139:1-3)

Too often we let these words describe God as the divine parole officer, and we conjure a God with the tracking abilities of a bloodhound and the affections of a boulder. This, I fear, is a particular temptation for Lutherans. Often we make faith an end in itself. These passionate texts convince us that faith means believing in a God who can love us in all the messy details. Think how different this psalm sounds when we see behind it God the worried mother or God the lover. Let these words wash over you, and feel in them God's love for you, specifically *you*.

> If I take the wings of the morning
>> and settle at the farthest limits of the sea,
> even there your hand shall lead me,
>> and your right hand shall hold me fast. (Psalm 139:9-10)

It feels like an embrace to me!

The Heart of Jesus

An old proverb claims that the eyes are the window to the soul. We often search people's eyes to gauge the state of their souls, to discern whether they are speaking truths or falsehoods, and to decide if they are teasing or serious, at peace or in turmoil. But how do we search the soul of God? How do we know the divine heart? The answer is easy. Look at Jesus. There we see the heart of God.

Jesus reads out God's EKG in his farewell discourse in the Gospel of John (14:1—17:26). Throughout his ministry, Jesus has addressed God with scandalous familiarity as "Abba." In this last teaching before his death, Jesus makes plain to his disciples what this means. Disciples need to cling to every word of this final farewell. Three verses in particular focus our attention.

The first verse is John 15:9: "As the Father has loved me, so I have loved you; abide in my love." With these words, Jesus makes clear God's relationship to him as being a father to a son. More powerfully, he reveals his father's love. As he shows us the father's love for his son, it suddenly becomes clear that we are all children of this father. We are all caught up in the embrace. He promises that this is a love we can "abide" in.

The word *abide* is no accident. The Greek *maneo* carries the con-
notation of resting in something that will hold you. Think of a trapeze
artist flying through the air. She may miss the catch, but she risks
everything because she knows the net is there. This is a good model for
discipleship, one that leans on the Father's love. We dare to love, and
we dare to live, because God is beneath us, cheering us on and ready to
catch us when we fall.

The second and third verses focus on the path of beloved disciples:
"This is my commandment, that you love one another as I have loved
you. No one has greater love than this, to lay down one's life for one's
friends" (John 15:12-13). Our task is simple: to love as we have been
loved. There is no way we can pay the Father back for the love the
Father has shown to us. Our duty and our delight is to pay it forward to
all the ends of the earth. Being loved so abundantly, we can spend that
love generously in a world that longs for a loving touch.

As if he were afraid disciples would miss the scandal of divine
love, Jesus contrasts the relationship between master and slave with
friendship and with the relationship between parents and children. If
the master/slave relationship characterizes how we relate to God, we
subordinate ourselves to a judging God. We respond with fear and an
eagerness to please. If friendship characterizes how we relate to God,
there is a different way of being together. There is an ease and mutual-
ity; we respond with love and the obedience born of love, not with fear
or servile submissiveness. After all, the Latin root of obedience means
"to listen for something—or someone." We obey God most when we
listen for his voice. Like the sheep of a good shepherd, we know the
sound of the shepherd's voice.

Now an earlier passage in John's Gospel makes different sense.
Jesus has identified himself as the good shepherd. As we just established, sheep know the very particular voice of their own shepherd—but
they do not recognize the voice of another shepherd. "When he has
brought out all his own, he goes ahead of them, and the sheep follow
him because they know his voice. They will not follow a stranger, but
they will run from him because they do not know the voice of strangers"
(John 10:4-5). After a long and drawn-out discourse on shepherding,

Jesus leaves no doubt as to his meaning: "I am the good shepherd. I know my own and my own know me" (John 10:14).

Taking Table Etiquette Seriously

There is an old and very popular Hallmark card that reads simply, "A friend is someone who likes you." That may be enough to say for us today, but in the ancient Near East, the card would have read differently: "A friend is someone you eat with." According to the Miss Manners of the ancient world, the people you ate with were your friends; your friends were the people you ate with. Dining together defined friendship.

This understanding of friendship lends new meaning to the gossip Jesus' critics tossed around: he is "a glutton, a drunkard, a friend of tax collectors and sinners!" (Matthew 11:19; Luke 7:34). . . . In their eyes, Jesus ate and drank with all the "wrong" kinds of people. There were all sorts of ways to qualify as the wrong kind of person.

People were measured to an impossible standard of conduct, and the standard was defined both religiously and politically. Failure to measure up marked you as a sinner. People would be doubly taxed at exorbitant rates by both the occupying Roman authorities and the temple priests. Failure to pay qualified you simultaneously as both sinner and criminal. Most despised of all were the tax collectors themselves, Jews drafted by need or circumstance into service by the occupying army to extort money out of their own countrymen.

Yet, these were Jesus' dining companions. He did not hang out with the "righteous," the pious Pharisees, Sadducees, and temple authorities. He did not care about their kind of righteousness. Instead, Jesus hung out with the "unrighteous." Having been spurned by the piety police, these folks yearned for righteousness. They literally "hungered and thirsted" for righteousness in the eyes of their world. They were truly satisfied, for they dined with righteousness itself: Jesus, the Righteous One of God. The promise of this beatitude was fulfilled in a simple meal.

Declaring his solidarity with the outcasts in the breaking of bread, Jesus left a powerful example with his disciples. He did not give food to the hungry, nor did he give drink to the thirsty. He ate with people, he drank with people, he was their friend. This simple gesture of table fellowship moves beyond charity, which is too often an exchange without intimacy between strangers. Sometimes a charitable gesture is anonymous, masking the identity of the giver entirely. In contrast, friendship asks to see the other's face and to hear the other's story. All this happens easily and naturally around a table.

Many years ago, a Roman Catholic bishop grasped the insight of Jesus' example. A young man, disaffected with organized religion, approached the bishop and demanded, "What must I do to be a Christian?" Without missing a beat, the bishop told him, "Go to Mass every day and work in a soup kitchen every week. That's what you must do to be a Christian." His advice states the two minimum daily requirements of discipleship, and they are both about meals. In eating and drinking the body and blood of Christ, we become members of his body. In breaking bread with the outcasts of our own day, we bring that sacred body into their midst. By eating and drinking with people, we pay the love of God forward into a world that longs for God's holy touch.

Beyond Charity and into Solidarity

The homeless population in Berkeley, California, is large because the weather is temperate, and the social services are abundant. Instead of complaining to city officials about the trash and the state of its flower beds, a local congregation decided to do something about the situation of men and women residing in the city's parks. They started serving meals. Once a month members gathered to prepare a meal together. They arrived early in the day to begin cooking. They set tables with tablecloths and utensils and brought out the church's finest china. They invited the homeless in as guests. After they served the meal, they sat down and ate with their guests, sharing table fellowship with them.

Over time once a month was not enough, so the congregation marshaled its resources to serve two meals a month. Soon other churches and synagogues in the neighborhood joined in. Bible study followed the meal, and as the years wore on, the members of these various congregations got to know those who hungered and thirsted for righteousness at their doorstep. And, they themselves were known by their guests. People who had been simply anonymous members of a category—that guy who sleeps under the church steps or that rich babe who drives the red Mercedes—became Patrick or Mary or Edward.

This is the stuff of discipleship: knowing as we have been known and loving as we have been loved. As Jesus demonstrated in his life and ministry, the love born of such fellowship happens around food. Before he died Jesus shared a final meal with his beloved disciples. And, as if that were not enough, he returned after the Resurrection to cook them breakfast, grilling fish for them along the shore (John 21). Sharing food and drink constitutes the kingdom. In doing this, we truly get a "foretaste of the feast to come."

There is a wonderful parable about table etiquette in heaven and hell. In both places huge tables are set, piled high with every imaginable delicacy. A place is set for everyone, but the utensils are foot-long spoons and forks. In hell, eating invites pandemonium, as the residents attempt to feed themselves, poking their utensils and elbows into each other's faces and ribs. In heaven, however, the meal proceeds with great joy and high delight: everyone feeds the person across the table and is fed in turn.

As we share food, we discover that we too are fed and in such gracious ways. Sometimes we do not even realize we are starving. This is the abundant life around God's table.

Questions for Reflection

1. How do you experience God's love? Count the ways. Now, how do you experience your love for God? Again, count the ways.

2. How do we fail at love in both great ways and in small ones? Think about how we fail at loving each other, how we fail at loving God, and how we fail at loving ourselves. Are there any similarities?

3. Think about God's love for us as passionate, romantic love. Is this a new thought? What does it mean for you?

4. Now think about our love for God in equally passionate, romantic terms. What does this open up for you?

5. How do you pay God's love forward?

For Further Reflection

Psalm 139

Listen to your favorite love song and notice how the beloved is described. You can almost touch her skin; you can smell the fragrance of his hair. Only a lover could come up with such description because only a lover pays such close attention. Love psalms are a lot like love songs, and Psalm 139 is a love psalm. God loves us enough to hang on our every word and to inquire about our every movement. Now, listen to Psalm 139 and catch the divine delight!

6

Mercy Made Real

Blessed are the merciful, for they will receive mercy.

—Matthew 5:7

I raced into a room where two teary-eyed girls were creating quite a ruckus. Each blubbered, "I didn't do it! She hit me! She hit me first!" It was impossible to figure out who started what. There was not time to sift through evidence anyway. First, I had to step in and stop the fighting that I knew would escalate.

The scenario is a familiar one to parents, social workers, and history buffs. It is an ancient pattern: I steal your sheep; you burn down my barn; I murder your sons; you kill all of my kin. The neighbors take sides, and before long the whole village is at war. Across centuries and cultures, the story repeats itself, between Montague and Capulet, Hatfield and McCoy, Palestinian and Jew, and Shiite, Sunni, and Kurd.

Sages have long counseled limit: an eye for an eye; a tooth for a tooth. What sounds like the brutal arithmetic of vengeance actually urges restraint: just *one* eye for an eye. I know if someone was to pluck out my eye, I would want that person's head on a platter. Instinct reacts to offense with overwhelming force, and the juggernaut of violence lurches forward.

What stops violence in its tracks? Mercy—mercy born of hard experience. The beatitude suggests that we know mercy because we have been given it. And, we have been given mercy because we need it. No one is an innocent victim on the journey of discipleship; God sees our impulse for revenge. Call it the "dark side" of the Golden Rule: "I want to do to you exactly what you have done to me—and then some!" "I want to hurt you as you have hurt me—and more!" Mercy confesses the instinct for retaliation and then steps away from it. But, just as a blessed person counts blessings and a resentful person nurses grudges, a merciful person remembers all the times he has been shown mercy. The merciful person spreads the love he has been given.

Mercy manifests itself as forgiveness, and forgiveness is the glue of human community. In the Lord's Prayer, Jesus invites disciples to ask their heavenly Father for what Christians need most for the journey of discipleship: food—"Give us this day our daily bread"; forgiveness—"Forgive us our sins"; and protection—"Deliver us from evil . . . . Lead us not into temptation." Forgiveness ranks right up there alongside the need for food and protection as something essential to Christian discipleship. Why?

Without mercy made manifest in the practice of forgiveness, disciples risk killing themselves and others in a cycle of unending violence. Without forgiveness, disciples would travel alone, alienated from others by slights and petty grievances—or worse. A single petition shows the path of reconciliation: "Forgive us our sins, as we forgive those who sin against us." In this beatitude, Jesus blesses those who forgive and also promises them forgiveness.

In this chapter, we examine mercy, the disposition that enables forgiveness. Mercy is an unnatural act: every instinct strains toward vengeance. It is an impossible demand, but the good news is that it is also a divine gift. Mercy may be contrary to the human spirit, but it is the essence of the divine spirit, as we see from the Hebrew scriptures. Jesus is God's mercy made flesh, and he shows us a way of forgiving even the unforgivable offenses. Finally, following his example, disciples become forgiven forgivers, showing mercy to a world that longs for it.

God's Mercy and Jonah's Protest

Our first house was a handyman's special, and the previous handyman had clearly given up. There were six different kinds of paneling in the basement, cracks in the stucco, paint peeling from the eaves, and doors that needed to be planed before they would close. We understood immediately that we were "home moaners." I described our domestic woes to a friend, who smiled, produced a business card, and said,

"Here's the person you need." The card simply read "Emmet Lynch, Fixer." There was a phone number at the bottom of the card.

A few days later, the Fixer showed up on our doorstep, dog in tow. He took a look around, filled a bowl of water for Emma, the dog, and went to work. Within about a week, it was all fixed, just as the card promised.

If the Old Testament showed us a business card for God, Exodus 34:6-7 would be on it:

> The LORD, the LORD, a God merciful and gracious, slow to anger, and abounding in steadfast love and faithfulness, keeping steadfast love for the thousandth generation, forgiving iniquity and transgression and sin, yet by no means clearing the guilty, but visiting the iniquity of the parents upon the children and the children's children, to the third and the fourth generation.

This business card declares God's ineffable mercy, God's commitment to trying again and again. Certainly there is judgment, and that judgment extends to "the third and the fourth generation." If this seems harsh, think of abused children. Too often, abusing parents were themselves abused. And behind them are their abusing parents, who were once upon a time abused as children. The cycle of violence rolls on and on. God's words seem less like a punishment than a simple statement of the human condition.

The divine condition is different. Look at God's mercy: it extends to "the thousandth generation." God's mercy reminds me of a mother running after a toddler who is chasing a ball. The ball bounces into a busy street, and the child goes after it. Just before he steps into traffic, the mother bolts from the house. In three quick steps, she is there. She scoops him up and out of harm's way. We have all seen something like this. It is a vivid analogy to a God who is "merciful and gracious." Scripture promises that God's mercy always outruns God's judgment. Mercy will trump judgment again and again.

Whenever our house needed repairs, my husband and I called Emmet, the Fixer. Sometimes we spoke of him as the Fixer, sometimes as Emmet. The two names were interchangeable. So it is with God in the Old Testament. Sometimes God is called "the LORD," and some-times God is referred to as "gracious and merciful." The words all speak of the same God. God leaves the same card throughout the Bible. The refrain of grace and mercy echoes throughout the biblical witness in psalmist and prophet alike (see, for example, Psalm 51:1, 86:15, 103:8, 111:4, 145:8; Jonah 4:2; Joel 2:13; Nehemiah 9:17). Indeed, whenever God's name comes up, the words "gracious and merciful" surface. Why do we need to be reminded so much? Why do we keep losing God's business card?

The story of Jonah offers an answer. God calls Jonah to preach repentance in the city of Nineveh, and the prophet refuses. Instead, he takes a ship to Tarshish, hoping to outrun his call. A great storm blows, threatening the lives of all on board. Suspecting the cause, Jonah con-fesses his situation to the sailors and tells them to throw him overboard. Notice that the sailors respond to Jonah's plight with mercy: they try to outrow the storm. When their efforts fail, they plead to Jonah's God to have mercy on them for what they are about to do, and then they pitch the reluctant prophet into the sea. The storm stops immediately, and a great fish swallows Jonah. From the belly of the fish, Jonah cries out to the Lord. The Lord has mercy on Jonah, and the great fish spews him out onto dry land. This time, Jonah goes to Nineveh, preaching repen-tance to the great city. His words so move the people that they repent of their evil ways, and the Lord prepares to save them. But, whereas Jonah had no objections to the Lord's great mercy on his behalf, he is angry that God would spare the Ninevites. He objects, asking to die a second time. Jonah wants mercy for himself but cannot stand to see it shown to others.

Jonah is a lot like us. Like in the parable of the tax collector and the Pharisee, how often have we spoken the words of the publican, "God, be merciful to me, a sinner!", and then thought, "But, gosh, isn't *he* a mess?!" It turns out that the publican and the Pharisee are not two dif-ferent people: they are two sides of our soul (Luke 18:9-14). We expect God to be merciful to us, but we reserve the right to judge everyone else. We lower the standards of divine mercy for ourselves, but we raise the bar for others. Again and again, the Old Testament reminds us that God is gracious and merciful. I like to think that if Jonah was a parent, he would have known better. Parents know all too well the ache of loving their children. Children never appreciate the depth of parental love until they have children of their own. Then they can look up from their longing and remember that they too have been so loved.

God loves each of us the way parents love their children. Indeed, one of the Hebrew words commonly used for "mercy," *rahamim*, comes from the word for "uterus," *rehem*. The prophet Isaiah likens divine mercy to a mother's love.

> But Zion said, "The LORD has forsaken me, my Lord has forgotten me." Can a woman forget her nursing child, or show no compassion for the child of her womb? Even these may forget, yet I will not forget you. (Isaiah 49:14-15)

Parents also love each child in a different way: Billy for his dreaminess, Richard for his spark, Catherine for her edge, and Mary for her sheer poetry. If parents are wise, they know that their children will never love them the way they love their children. It does not matter, though. They only hope that their children will love *their* children with that same unconditional and attentive love. In the same way, God loves us the way a parent loves each child: Susan for her fine judgment, Bill for his generous spirit, Erin for her sense of humor. In addition to love, God *delights* in us—for some of the wildest reasons: Lisa for her love of chocolate, Mark for his break dancing, Jane for the way she wears purple. God both loves and delights in each of us. We can never pay back such a love as God's; the only response is to pay it forward by being merciful to others.

Mercy Made Flesh

A child awoke at night convinced that monsters lurked in her bedroom. She ran into her parents' bedroom. Her mother calmed her and led her back into her own room, where she turned on a light and reassured the child by saying, "You're not alone. Remember that God is always here with you." "I know," the child responded, "but I need some-one with some skin." Jesus is God with some skin. More importantly, Jesus is God's mercy made flesh.

Jesus shares God's mercy recklessly, spreading compassion to the crowds that gathered for healing (Mark 6:34; Matthew 14:14), healing blind men begging along the roadside (Luke 18:35-43), and casting out demons (Mark 5:1-13). There is no way these people could repay Jesus for the mercy he had shown them. In each instance, he urges them to share the mercy they have been shown: "Go home to your friends, and tell them how much the Lord has done for you, and what mercy he has shown you" (Mark 5:19). Mercy, like manna, cannot be hoarded. It has to be spread around, lest it too become stale. Mercy moves around, and those who have received it then also share it.

The quality of mercy comes to the fore in a parable central to Jesus' ministry, the parable of the Good Samaritan (Luke 10:25-37). The para-ble is so familiar to us that we miss the questions that prompt it. The law-yer's first question to Jesus is a *what* question: "What must I do to inherit eternal life?" Jesus responds with a *what* question of his own: "What is written in the law?" (10:25-26) The lawyer probes further, posing this time a who question: "And who is my neighbor?" (10:29) Whatever the lawyer expected as an answer, he must have been surprised.

Jesus launches into a parable that would have deeply offended its hearers. Samaritans were never seen as "good," but always as "outsiders" and most often as "bad." Furthermore, the "good" people in the story, a priest and a Levite, were the "best" people in Jewish society. Yet, they ignored a man dying in their midst. As Jesus ends his story, it becomes clear that he has not addressed the lawyer's question at all. The lawyer had asked the wrong question. The question Jesus answers with this unsettling parable is a *how* question: "How can *I* be a neighbor?" And the answer to this question is to show mercy. Mercy sums up the nature of discipleship.

Mercy means following the example of the Samaritan and spread-ing mercy as he did. Jesus does not say, "Go and do exactly the same thing." Nor does he say, "Go and do whatever you want." Rather, disciples are to pattern their lives on the mercy shown in this story, a compassion that responds to another person in appropriate and loving ways. Mercy may mean different things in different situations: here a casserole, there an invitation to lunch or dinner, somewhere else the simple gift of sitting still in solidarity with someone who is lonely. Jesus' response frees us to love as the situation demands.

What if we cannot muster mercy? Is forgiveness always possible? What happens when love is beyond our human capacities? The answer to these questions lies in the Crucifixion. Too often, Jesus' words from the cross play with hallelujah choruses in the background; we skip ahead to Easter. But, in fact, Jesus felt himself abandoned by friends, followers, and even his beloved Father. He stared into the abyss of evil. His choice was clear: join it or defy it. In the depths of his pain, he defied evil with a gesture of mercy: "Father, forgive them; for they do not know what they are doing" (Luke 23:34).

We like to think that Jesus spoke with compassion, but he may well have spit these words out. I imagine he was human enough to feel all the recrimination to which he was entitled, and I imagine he struggled with the unnatural character of forgiveness just like the rest of us. Whether his tone was one of mercy or recrimination, the words themselves shock us. Notice that Jesus does not say, "*I* forgive you; *I* have mercy upon you." The man who taught his disciples to love their enemies could not measure up himself. He could not forgive all of this evil on his own, and so he called out to the source of all mercy: "*Father,* forgive them." With these words, he asked God to forgive what he could not.

Jesus stands as a stunning example of the reach of divine mercy. When our frail powers of forgiving fail us, we can ask God to forgive our enemies until we can forgive them on our own. In a letter to his friend Malcolm, C.S. Lewis recalled the cruelty of a schoolmaster who had for years inflicted physical and emotional abuse on his students. The schoolmaster had long since died, but the memory of abuse lingered. Lewis turned the matter over to prayer. Writing to Malcolm, he observed the following: "Last week while at prayer, I suddenly discovered—or felt as if I did—that I had really forgiven someone I had been trying to forgive for over thirty years. Trying and praying that I might."[1] Like Jesus, Lewis called on the abundance of divine mercy to help him when his own powers fell short. Eventually, forgiveness found him. Forgiveness will find us, as well, as we pray daily and fervently: "Forgive us our sins, as we forgive those who sin against us."

Forgiven Forgivers

There is a story about a prisoner in the Tower of London who after many years was released by royal pardon. But when the warden unlocked the door to his cell, the prisoner did not budge. "The king has had mercy on you. You're free," the warden said. "Yes," the prisoner replied, "but I know the world of this cell. I know not what lies beyond it." The prisoner chose the known cell over an unknown freedom. His story sheds light on Scriptures in which familiarity wins out again and again over the wild world of God's mercy. This is evident with the Israelites when they are a few weeks into the wilderness and begin to yearn for the "fleshpots" of Egypt, where they had just been freed from their oppression. God's mercy seems hard to stomach.

Peter's encounter with divine mercy stuns him. He has been out all night fishing and has caught nothing. Then when Jesus urges him to throw out his nets again, Peter can barely pull them in, as they are so full of fish. He looks at Jesus with sudden recognition and certain self-revulsion: "Go away from me, Lord, for I am a sinful man!" (Luke 5:8). The encounter with divine mercy is too much for him, and he grasps wildly for the familiar. Jesus reels him in, and Peter will fish for people, spreading divine mercy still further.[2]

Peter is the one who prompts a parable about mercy, a commentary on this beatitude. He asks Jesus a question about forgiveness, and like the lawyer who heard the parable of the Good Samaritan, he wants to quantify it: "How often should I forgive?" (Matthew 18:21-35). He wants numbers, and Jesus gives him an impossible one. Then, he tells Peter *how* he should forgive, not *how often*. The parable tells of a servant who receives mercy but will not give it. The servant is a latter-day Jonah. Jesus concludes the parable with a statement on the quality, not the quantity, of forgiveness: "So my heavenly Father will also do to every one of you, if you do not forgive your brother or sister from your heart" (Matthew 18:35). The story states the identity of disciples: forgiven forgivers. We show mercy because we have so richly received it.

A final encounter fixes our standing as forgiven forgivers. Jesus was crucified between two common criminals. The disciples had abandoned him. After reports of Jesus' resurrection, the disciples went into hiding. They were probably more frightened of running into Jesus than the Roman or Jewish authorities. They had merely irritated the authorities, but they had betrayed Jesus. They locked themselves in a room, and suddenly Jesus appeared among them, mercy in their midst. "Peace be with you," their resurrected Lord said (John 20:19). The words were so unexpected that Jesus had to repeat himself. With these words, Jesus gave the disciples what they most needed but could not ask for: mercy. Then, immediately following these words of reconciliation, he entrusts them with a ministry of mercy: "If you forgive the sins of any, they are forgiven them; if you retain the sins of any, they are retained" (John 20:23).

As the disciples moved out into the world, that memory shaped their ministries of mercy. Every encounter with a sinner seeking forgiveness reminded them of Jesus' own lavish mercy. Every absolution they gave repeated the words that freed their own guilty consciences: "Peace be with you." The disciples become forgiven forgivers.

Mercy's Practice

Forgiveness is the practice of mercy. This practice plays out a divine drama in three acts: repenting, remembering, and reconciling.

The first step in forgiveness enables disciples to turn away from violence. As we pray, "Forgive us our sins," we remind ourselves that we too are sinners in need of repentance. No matter how unjust our suffering is, we yearn to return evil for evil. By repenting of our own capacity for violence, we refuse retaliation and embrace forgiveness instead. Repentance is the first act in the drama of forgiveness, and revenge is its chief temptation.

The second step in forgiveness overturns the popular counsel to forgive and forget. Trying to forget injustice only fuels passive aggression and denial. Memory reopens an injury, but it also underscores a daily need to turn consciously away from avenging it. In remembering our own tendency toward revenge and our own desperate need for repentance, we open ourselves to be re-membered in the body of Christ. Remembering is the second act in the drama of forgiveness, and amnesia is its chief temptation.

Reconciliation is the final step in forgiveness, enabling disciples to embrace Jesus' most difficult command: "Love your enemies and pray for those who persecute you" (Matthew 5:44). Recrimination is the temptation in this case because it blocks reconciliation, refusing solidarity and choosing alienation.

Repenting, remembering, and reconciling: the practice of mercy is a divine drama in three acts. Mastery of these three steps, no matter how many times we take them, comes slowly. For that reason, we pray for grace, petitioning daily: "Forgive us our sins, as we forgive those who sin against us." We wait for the miracle that is forgiveness.

Questions for Reflection

1. Jonah is a great biblical example of someone who covets God's mercy for himself but does not want to share it with the Ninevites. Do you have any examples of this that are closer to home?

2. Have you ever felt the kind of gut-wrenching sympathy that the Samaritan felt when he saw the beaten man? Share some stories.

3. What are your experiences of forgiving and being forgiven? Is it hard to see yourself as a forgiven forgiver? Why or why not?

4. Have you ever needed to ask for God's help to forgive someone else or to be forgiven yourself?

For Further Reflection

Psalm 51

This psalm opens up the season of Lent, for it expresses the anguish of a penitent. Here, sin is more than a matter of misdeeds; sin reflects the falseness of "living a lie." So, the psalmist pleads for a "clean heart . . . and . . . a new and right spirit" (v. 10). Yet, nothing—not even sin—can erase the image in which we were made. We are hardwired for praise, and the psalmist remains convinced that if we let the Lord open our lips, what will pour forth is blessing: "O Lord, open my lips, and my mouth will declare your praise" (v. 15). Think of the many other kinds of words that open your lips, such as words of anger, frustration, and judgment, and let God open your lips. Live as you were created: hardwired for blessing.

7

Pure in Heart; Rich in Vision

Blessed are the pure in heart, for they will see God.

—Matthew 5:8

I remember the delicious pleasure of seeing a movie in the middle of a weekday afternoon. I stepped out of the theater into a bright afternoon sun—and scurried back into the darkness. The light was so bright that it hurt after the cool darkness of the theater. But my life was in the sunlit world, and so I strapped on sunglasses, took a deep breath, and headed out into the brightness.

Seeing God dazzles us in different ways, but the reaction is the same. We want to duck back into the darkness, possibly forever, or at least until our eyes adjust. The prospect of seeing God terrifies more than it delights, and this beatitude tells us why. Our hearts are not pure, and, therefore, we cannot stand to gaze at what we most desire.

I want to back into this beatitude, exploring spiritual myopia, or the things that blur our vision. Just as Jesus healed the blind, he heals us. He repairs our sight in two ways, by restoring our vision and by being himself, "the image of the invisible God" (Colossians 1:15). When we see Jesus, the scales fall from our eyes. When our hearts are made clean through the sacrament of his body and blood, Jesus enables us to be who we are: creatures fashioned in the image of God. We become "stewards of God's mysteries" (1 Corinthians 4:1). After all, what are prophets but seers, literally people who see into God's future. The cry of disciples is the proclamation of Mary Magdalene: "I have seen the Lord" (John 20:18). The practice of the Lord's Supper offers us ongoing eye exercises, training our vision on the God in our midst.

Seeing God—and Living

"You are what you eat!" proclaim the great gurus of food. They seek to recruit us to one of any number of food regimes so that we can be justified by diet. An ample-bodied Lutheran friend of mine simply laughs at their righteousness. "I'll stick to faith," she says, slapping a well-padded thigh.

The biblical version would read, "You are what you look at." Ancient people theorized that two fires illumine the world for each of us: the fire that is the sun and the fire that is in the eye. The sun dispels darkness, but the fire in the eye illuminates whatever the eye focuses on, casting light on it like the concentrated beam of a flashlight. Think of a deer caught in the headlights of a car and how iridescent the animal's eyes are. This is what the ancients were talking about.

We need both fires to see. Without the fire of the sun, we would dwell in darkness; without the fire in the eyes, we would be blind. The two form a bridge of light, and knowledge of the world streams across the bridge to enter the body. Everything seen is imprinted on the heart. People become what they behold. For the ancients, seeing was as much a spiritual process as a physical one.

Not surprisingly, people learned to be careful of what they looked at. Looks could kill—and quite often did. In fourth-century North Africa, Saint Augustine wrote of his friend Alypius, who could not take his eyes off the violence of the arena. Augustine described the effects: "He was struck in the soul by a wound graver than the gladiator in his body, whose fall caused the uproar. . . . As soon as he saw the blood, he at once drank in savagery and did not turn away. His eyes were riveted. He imbibed madness. Without any awareness of what was happening to him, he found delight in the murderous context and was inebriated by bloodthirsty pleasure."[1] Augustine describes addiction in all its compulsive splendor.

Then and now, violence enthralls us. The television and movie industry understands this well. We are more like Lot's wife than we would like to admit (Genesis 19:26). Given the opportunity to gaze into a future of freedom or watch Sodom burn, she turned toward the burning city. Trained on a steady diet of violence in both movies and the media, we might do the same.

We talk about "a penetrating gaze," but in the biblical world, all gazes penetrated the beholder. What people looked at shaped their hearts and their desires. Maybe it all started with Adam and Eve in the garden. After that first bite of the forbidden fruit, "the eyes of both were opened, and they knew that they were naked" (Genesis 3:7). We have been looking at ourselves ever since. We cannot see much with that kind of obstruction. What blocks our view of God and everything else? We do, and often quite willfully.

There is another reason for spiritual shortsightedness. Looking at God is a dangerous matter. In one of his books, *Anil's Ghost*, Canadian author Michael Ondaatje introduces the reader to Ananda, who is last in the line of artists appointed to paint faces on statues of the larger-than-life Buddhas worshiped throughout his native country of Sri Lanka.[2] The artist paints the eyes of the statues last. He does this by looking into a mirror and working over his shoulder. Buddhist spirituality warns its practitioners that when the eyes of the Buddha are finished, the spirit of the image comes alive. The Buddha suddenly sees—and being beheld by a Buddha is a dangerous thing. No one can stare straight into the eyes of the Buddha at close range and live.

This danger is also evident in the Hebrew scriptures. Jacob cannot quite believe his encounter with God at Peniel, and he marvels, "For I have seen God face to face, and yet my life is preserved" (Genesis 32:30). God gets the message, though. God shields Moses from direct sight: "You cannot see my face; for no one shall see me and live" (Exodus 33:20). In this incident that fascinated Martin Luther millennia later, Moses saw God's "back" instead (Exodus 33:23). Seen through the lens of this beatitude, however, the encounter captures our attention for other reasons. God singles out Moses for a relationship that begins with a burning bush, deepens throughout the wilderness wanderings, and weathers whatever it was that happened at Meribah when Moses struck a rock to produce water.[3]

Seeing God is not something Moses sought. But, God had chosen him, and part of divine choice includes the kind of mutual revelation that happens between close friends. Shortly after the burning bush encounter, God tells Moses, "I am the LORD. I appeared to Abraham,

Isaac, and Jacob as God Almighty, but by my name 'The LORD' I did not make myself known to them" (Exodus 6:2-3). God shows himself to Moses as "the LORD," and Scripture signals their intimacy visually.

Lovers and close friends call each other nicknames; they read each other with a glance. So it is with God and Moses. They seal their relationship with mutual naming and, more important, mutual beholding. They look at each other without flinching. While the bush burned, Moses simply took off his shoes, stood his ground, and looked.

Most of us would run in terror at the prospect of seeing God. Indeed, the Israelites could not stand to look at Moses after he had been with God. Even the reflected light of a divine encounter was too much for them. They put a veil on him to dim the wattage.[4] However, the Israelites could stand to look at a golden calf; they even gazed upon a bronze serpent when their lives depended on it (Numbers 21:9). But, they did not want to see God face-to-face.

We are not unlike our forefathers and foremothers in the wilderness. Goodness is too much for us sometimes; we prefer the sitcoms. With the psalmist, we say we long to see God's face. In truth, we run from divine goodness, preferring darkness to that great light.

What we look at has the power to transform or deform us. Perhaps the apostle Paul thinks along the lines of the ancients when he counsels the Christians at Philippi: "Finally, beloved, whatever is true, whatever is honorable, whatever is just, whatever is pure, whatever is pleasing, whatever is commendable, if there is any excellence and if there is anything worthy of praise, think about these things" (Philippians 4:8). Like Augustine with his friend Alypius, Paul knew that we become what we attend to.

Image of the Invisible God

In my city homeless women and men line the downtown streets, begging for handouts from passersby. Reacting to the situation, the chamber of commerce worries about attracting local business, the mayor worries about providing social services, the health department worries about sanitation. My church decided to stop worrying and do something. It offered a weekly meal and a more formal sit-down dinner once a month. Other churches took notice and began similar ministries. Tensions eased; tempers calmed. The coordinator of the program said, "We just decided to stop thinking of the homeless as a 'problem.' They are people, just like us. Just like us, they want to be seen." The "problem" for homeless people is visibility. People walk past them as if they are not there. People deliberately refuse to see.

The author of the letter to the Colossians tells us that Jesus is "the image of the invisible God" (Colossians 1:15). Jesus is the image of the God who told Moses, "You cannot see my face . . . and live." Yet, I suspect people regarded Jesus in much the same way as they regard a homeless man on the streets of Berkeley: ignored as long as he was quiet; locked up if he made his presence known. And Jesus always made his presence known—touching, healing, and forgiving. Time and again, he healed people with the words "Your sins are forgiven you." The absolution seems unfairly to equate disease and sin, but ancient superstition understood disease and disability as the result of someone's transgression. Because of this ungrounded fear, healthy people avoided sick people, ignoring them if they could and crossing to the other side of the road if they had to.[5] These actions made the sick feel untouchable, even invisible. But Jesus saw them; he touched them. More than that, he erased the fear that they had somehow brought all of this onto themselves. He knew that sick people who were suddenly healed would find themselves face-to-face with God. Afraid they would turn away from so much goodness, he assured them in advance that "your sins are forgiven."

Read another healing story through the lens of this beatitude: the story of the man born blind (John 9:1-38). Pharisees and disciples alike attributed this man's blindness to sin. The only question was whose sin: his? his parents? But Jesus ruled out their questions. No sin caused the man's blindness. Jesus then healed him; the man could see.

Look through the eyes of this man, born blind and suddenly seeing. The first thing he sees is the face of the living God. More like Moses than Peter, the man stands his ground, staring into the face of God. He does not need to hide from view; he simply does what Jesus tells him. He goes to the pool of Siloam and washes the mud off his eyes.

Most healing stories end with the healing, but this one keeps the cameras rolling. The people who witnessed the miracle track down the man, demanding again and again that he recount his healing. Again like Moses, the man stands his ground, telling them twice that Jesus put mud on his eyes, he washed, and now he sees (John 9:11, 15). The people ask him a third time, and the man challenges them: "I have told you already, and you would not listen. Why do you want to hear it again? Do you also want to become his disciples?" (9:27) When the people try to squeeze from him a confession of Jesus as the Messiah, the man stands his ground again: "If this man were not from God, he could do nothing" (9:33). In their frustration, the people drive him out.

When Jesus finds the man, he asks him if he believes in the Son of Man, and the man asks, "Who is he, sir? Tell me, so that I may believe in him" (9:36). Now, if the man were speaking to a pastor or a scholar, these words might be the invitation for a long discussion on Christology. But, the man is speaking with Jesus, the Christ of God. Jesus does not need to offer any long-winded explanations of his own identity; he does not need to justify himself. Jesus simply says, "You have seen him." Seeing is believing. The man speaks the words that his actions have shown all along: "Lord, I believe."

In light of this beatitude, this story of healing takes on new dimensions. A man born blind suddenly sees. Just as suddenly, he is catapulted from invisibility to uncomfortable visibility. Against a barrage of antagonistic questions, he stands his ground. In a flurry of provocations, he holds firm. He knows who he is; he knows what happened to him. He even has a hunch who did it.

The man born blind is a powerful center of gravity in this story. If anyone has a pure heart, it is this man. Truly, he has seen God. The promise of the beatitude, "for they will see God," and the condition that prompts it, "pure in heart," are one.

Jesus Tries Again with Us

What we know of God, we know from God's Son, Jesus. Jesus alone has seen God, as John's Gospel makes clear: "Not that anyone has seen the Father except the one who is from God; he has seen the Father"

(6:46). Not only has Jesus seen God, but Jesus also reveals God to us in ways that we can stand. In Jesus, we see the face of the living God.

Still, it is not always easy to look. As we have seen, disciples get in the way of their own view. They also paper over the face of God with their own projections. We see this explicitly in a pivotal exchange between Jesus and Peter in the Gospel of Mark. The eighth chapter is the hinge of Mark's Gospel. Before the conversation with the disciples at Caesarea Philippi, there are miracles and healings; after that encounter, they almost cease. Jesus sets his face toward Jerusalem. The atmosphere of the entire Gospel alters.

In this chapter, Jesus pauses to take the pulse of his ministry. He asks the disciples, "Who do people say that I am?" They report what they have seen and heard: Elijah, John the Baptist, one of the prophets. These answers signal to Jesus the deepest longings of the people.

- Elijah—According to Jewish legend, Elijah would return just before "the day of the Lord." In Jesus' time, "the day of the Lord" was widely understood to signal liberation from the occupying Roman army in Palestine. If Jesus were Elijah, liberation loomed in the immediate future.
- John the Baptist—John the Baptist had been a beloved preacher, opening to all the way of repentance and the forgiveness of sins. But John met an untimely and unjust end at the hands of Herod, and the people missed him sorely. If Jesus were John the Baptist, the people's beloved master would have returned, and his promise would be theirs.
- One of the prophets—The voice of prophecy had long been silent in Israel. Though the people had resisted the prophets when they were alive, many in Jesus' time felt that the silence of prophecy in Israel signaled that God no longer cared about them. If Jesus were one of the prophets, God still cared.

People see in Jesus figures such as Elijah, John the Baptist, and one of the prophets. They project onto him their deepest longings. But, they have not really seen him. Then, Jesus asks the people who know him best, "Who do you say that I am?" Peter bursts out impetuously, "You are the Messiah."

According to Jewish expectation, the Messiah would rise up from the desert, liberating the chosen people from foreign occupation with military might. Peter hopes Jesus is that kind of revolutionary leader. He probably even sees himself as second in command of the revolutionary militia. But what follows shows that Peter has not seen Jesus clearly. Instead of offering a battle plan, Jesus describes a passion story. The Son of Man will suffer, die, and after three days rise again.

This is not a story of which Peter wants to be a part. He signed up for a different movie with a different soundtrack. This is not the way he wants to see Jesus; this is not the way he wants to see himself. Peter takes Jesus aside and tries to silence him. Jesus responds sharply. He calls Peter "Satan" and puts him in his place: "Get behind me." Not even the people closest to Jesus have really seen him.

Yet, two things give hope to disciples, both then and now. First, Jesus does not banish Peter. He could have said, "Get lost." Jesus puts Peter in his place, but that place is not the outer darkness. Second, the context of this exchange signals Jesus' commitment to try again with Peter—and with us. Immediately preceding this exchange is the healing of another blind man. Jesus' healing touch does not work the first time around. The man opens his eyes to see people, "but they look like trees, walking" (Mark 8:24). Jesus simply tries again, and the second time the man sees.

The placement of this healing story is no coincidence: a failed, first-time healing prefaces the story of a failed, first-time disciple. Jesus tries again with Peter. And, if Jesus tries again with Peter, he will try again with us.

Seeing in the Breaking of the Bread

These days, some people like to say they are spiritual, but not religious. Alienated by the institutional church, many people regard themselves as "recovering Christians." Been there, done that. One woman told me with great satisfaction, "I find God everywhere: in a beautiful sunset or just walking along the beach." "Great," I responded. "When was the last time you walked along a beach?"

Not that I do not appreciate beauty, but I cannot always find time for a trip to the beach. More important, I need practice in how to look for God. There are a lot of "spirits" out there, not all of them benign. How do we know we are connecting with the good ones? How do we know when we are connecting with the Spirit of God? Suppose the ancients were right: we are what we look at. How do we know we are paying attention to the right kinds of things?

Christians connect with the Spirit of God in Jesus Christ. We circle back to the Lord's Supper, where once again disciples recognize Jesus in the breaking of the bread (Luke 24:31, 35). Here, we see the invisible God made visible in ordinary elements of bread and wine. As we keep coming back to the Lord's Supper, we become what we eat: the body of Christ in the world.

Eucharistic living has two implications for discipleship. First, if we are what we eat, then all who feed on Christ become one. Paul's words are familiar: "There is no longer Jew or Greek, there is no longer slave or free, there is no longer male and female; for all of you are one in Christ Jesus" (Galatians 3:28). But, listen to Paul from another point-of-view, a strictly dietary one. Jew and Greek, slave and free, men and women: each of these groups participated in very different dietary regimes, some by necessity, some by choice, and some by religious conviction. No wonder the first fights in these earliest Christian communities were about food! Yet, one meal drew everyone together: the Lord's Supper. This meal slowly altered all of them, as they ate the same food and drank the same drink, hardwiring them into one body. We are the visible presence of the invisible God in the world.

Second, eucharistic living means that we are to bear the blessing of that meal to others. In the end, the Lord's Supper is not about eating food, but sharing it. We do not swarm the altar, tear off a chunk of bread, wash it down with a slug of wine, and make way for the next hungry mouth. Rather, the celebrant breaks the bread, blesses it, and shares it with someone else. The sharing goes on until everyone is fed. Jesus' meal sets in motion a miraculous chain of events that continues until we share food with the hungriest mouth in the world. Shared food nourishes disciples along the way; sharing food becomes our mission.

Like the loaves and fish at the miraculous feedings, the food we share will have no end, for we share the endless goodness of Christ.

Questions for Reflection

1. What do you look at? What do you think about? What worries wake you at three in the morning? What rents space in your head? What fixes your attention, like a fly caught in flypaper?

2. If there was a Twelve-Step group like Violence Addicts Anonymous, St. Augustine's friend Alypius would be there. Consider all the violence that television and the Internet beam into our homes. Is Alypius' addiction so different from our own?

3. How do you see God in the breaking of the bread? And, how do you share that meal with those people who are hungry for it?

For Further Reflection

Psalm 27

"Of whom shall I be afraid?" (v. 1) I hear a shaky confidence in these words. There are many things to be afraid of. Enemies abound; evil looms on all sides. Is God even paying attention? We should hear both desperation and exasperation behind the words "Hear, O Lord, when I cry aloud" (v. 7). The psalmist shouts for God's attention: "Where are you?! Listen up!" He fears God has hidden from him: "Do not hide your face from me" (v. 9).

If you want to know the meaning of "the outer darkness," think of it as a place where God's face is hidden. No light reaches that place. The psalmist asks for eye exercises so that he might gaze on the face of God. He begs to be taught in divine ways, to be led in divine wisdom. Then, and only then, will he be able to see "the goodness of the Lord in the land of the living" (v. 13).

8

Making Peace and Being Peace

Blessed are the peacemakers, for they will be called children of God.
                                                    —Matthew 5:9

An old rancher, knowing the end was near, summoned his family to his bedside. "Do you all want to keep on fighting, or shall we try to get along for once?" he asked. The words that the family inscribed on his headstone reminded them of his deepest and dying wish: "Rest in peace."

Many headstones bear these weighty words; they cover a multitude of situations. They may signal release from a wasting disease that made someone's final months miserable. Or, they might mark escape from a series of unresolved domestic conflicts that brought an embittered family to the funeral. Or, they might witness to the simple truth that living well is both a gift and an uphill battle. "Rest in peace." We think this is our final blessing on the dead.

I fear we misread our own inscriptions. These are not words we speak to the dead; they are words the dead speak to the living. "Rest in peace" sums up their final counsel to those of us left behind. Imagine what these bones would say if they could speak: "We have seen it all, and we know that peace is the only way to live. Resist violence, reconcile with your enemies, and love without measure." These are the last words of the dead to the living, and they challenge us to spend our days making peace.

Peace is God's deepest desire for us, and the Creator wove it into the fabric of creation. That incident with Adam, Eve, and the forbidden fruit ripped apart the relationships creation established, leaving us with a threadbare understanding of peace as simply the absence of conflict. Yet, throughout Scripture, there are hints at the fullness of God's intended *shalom*, a thick version of peace that promises not simply the end of war, but rich participation in God's justice. *Shalom* is a peace that makes for justice, a rich peace that reaches toward the right relationships intended in creation. Family values among the children of God demand making peace and doing justice.

Shalom: The Peace We Rest In

I bristled when the man offered me the peace of Christ. I knew he did not like me, and I feared his troubled soul. I had heard him preach many times, and every sermon featured a violent illustration: keying a car, breaking a picture frame, throwing a chair across the chancel. Stunned by these bursts of negative energy, listeners could barely discern the intended gospel message. Now, this angry man offered me the peace of Christ.

It is not a gesture you can decline: "No thanks, not today." It is also not something you can negotiate: "Can I get that in writing?" I answered by the book: "And also with you." Because I had seen hints of trouble, I believed all the more firmly that *Christ's* peace could be our only authentic bond. I knew that Christ's peace would somehow right a troubled relationship. Christ's was the peace that would do justice.

That trust is rightly placed. The prophet Isaiah proclaimed not simply the end of war, but the dawning of abundance. Peace would come as a person, a "Wonderful Counselor, Mighty God, Everlasting Father, Prince of Peace" (Isaiah 9:6). Christ is the peace of God, and that peace permeates every page of Scripture. The Hebrew scriptures call that peace *shalom*.

Too often, we define *shalom* by what it is not: it is not war, nor famine, nor enmity. The list expands infinitely, covering conflicts great and small, from a slight that lies festering in memory, to the genocide in Darfur, and to the nameless and shadowy enemy behind the War on Terror. Add your own frustrations. Then, imagine them gone. Finally, understand that your list does not begin to embrace God's peace. All this is *shalom*-lite, a diet version of God's peace.

Biblical *shalom* describes a goodness that can barely be dreamed, though the prophet Isaiah gives it his best shot:

The wolf shall live with the lamb,
   the leopard shall lie down with the kid,
The calf and the lion and the fatling together,
   and a little child shall lead them.
The cow and the bear shall graze,
   their young shall lie down together;
   and the lion shall eat straw like the ox.
The nursing child shall play over the hole of the asp,
   and the weaned child shall put its hand on the adder's den.
They will not hurt or destroy
   on all my holy mountain;
For the earth will be full of the knowledge of the LORD
   as the waters cover the sea. (Isaiah 11:6-9)

As Isaiah's vision unfolds, the earth traces its steps back into the Garden of Eden. God turns relationships that were broken by the Fall back to their intended harmony. In restoring these relationships, God gives a peace that does justice.

Finally, biblical peace plays out not just in a vision, but in the concrete. It becomes incarnate; it resides in the particulars. Neither abstract concept nor fuzzy good feeling, *shalom* comes to us in the fabric of our relationships with people we know and in the world in which we live. *Shalom* signals God's promise that the curses of Genesis 3 will not be God's final judgment. The psalmist envisions a time when "love and truth will meet; justice and peace will kiss" (Psalm 85:11, NAB). *Shalom* fuses together justice and peace. The biblical story of Ruth, a Moabite woman, is a stunning cameo of *shalom*. Enemies are reconciled, curses are turned into blessing, and a peace that does justice is made.

Ruth: Making Peace in the Midst of Conflict

The book of Ruth interrupts a tale of political turmoil with a love story. The final words of the book of Judges, just before the book of Ruth, declare the end of civic morality in Israel: "In those days there was no king in Israel; all the people did what was right in their own eyes" (Judges 21:25). The implication is clear. After they get rid of their judges, the people not only do not *do* what is right; they do not even *know* what is right.

Then, immediately after the book of Ruth, 1 Samuel narrates the people's demand to have a king "like other nations" (8:5). The implication is clear here, as well. They think God is not "king" enough for them. Sandwiched in between the books of Judges and 1 Samuel, the book of Ruth seems to interrupt this conflict with a story of tender devotion.

But is Ruth's story really the shift from the political to the personal that it seems to be? Perhaps not. While others make trouble, Ruth makes peace. Her story offers a just alternative to the people's warlike souls, and her example demonstrates love's power over hatred and enmity.

A Serbian-American once recounted his parents' old neighborhood by the steel mill. Serbians lived on one side of the street, Croatians on the other. Even in the new country, these feuding groups stuck together. The man explained why: "We knew who we were by knowing who we were against." That ancient hatred gave new immigrants an old identity, something with which they were familiar. Their hatred defined them.

Fourth-century theologian Saint Augustine observed that our enemies will not get us, but our enmity will. He knew what he was talking about. As he died, barbarian armies were streaming across the coast of North Africa. Yet, Augustine knew the enemy was even closer than the troops storming the gates of his city. The most dangerous enemy lies buried in our warlike souls. Underneath hatred lives fear, a fear that defines us.

What a contrast to the story of Ruth! Ruth was a Moabite woman, and relations between the Hebrew people and the Moabites were every bit as tense as those between the Serbians and the Croatians. Things were strained at best, but they were usually antagonistic. Isaiah caught the enmity in his words: "Let Moab wail, let everyone wail for Moab" (Isaiah 16:7). Famine had forced the Hebrew Elimelech, his wife Naomi, and their two sons, Mahlon and Chilion, to move into Moabite territory. The sons took Moabite wives, Ruth being one of them, perhaps to speed their assimilation. Within ten years, however,

Elimelech and his sons were dead. Naomi "was left without her two sons and her husband," the text tells us (Ruth 1:5). She was also left in enemy territory.

Naomi's lament of her lot to her daughters-in-law bears scrutiny in a study on the beatitudes. Naomi considers herself cursed, not blessed: "The hand of the LORD has turned against me" (1:13). Even after Ruth declares her devotion and goes with her mother-in-law to Bethlehem, Naomi clings to her shame. Like my friend's old neighbors, she sticks to her old script. It is familiar; it is all she has. Naomi reenters Bethlehem announcing to all who will listen, "Call me no longer Naomi, call me Mara, for the Almighty has dealt bitterly with me" (1:20). Her bitterness is more familiar to her than Ruth's devotion. Naomi lets fear define her.

What was going through Ruth's mind as she listened to her mother-in-law's laments? She must have felt overwhelmed, under-noticed, and afraid. Naomi was a stranger in Moab, and now Ruth is a stranger in Bethlehem. Her mother-in-law seems unaware of Ruth's sacrifice and unappreciative of her love. Nonetheless, Ruth settles into Bethlehem, her resolve unaltered, "at the beginning of the barley harvest" (1:22).

Now, the blessings begin. For the rest of the book, blessings replace the first chapter's laments. We need both hands to count them all:

- Boaz blesses the reapers in his field, one of whom is Ruth (2:4).
- Boaz blesses Ruth with an extra portion of grain (2:14).
- Boaz again blesses Ruth for coming to him at night as he sleeps on the threshing room floor (3:10).
- The women of the village bless the God who has blessed Naomi (4:14).
- Even Naomi's attitude improves, and she blesses Boaz for his care (2:20).

What happened? Ruth simply acted out of love in a situation of conflict. That changed everything. It made for a peace that does justice.

Previously, Ruth disobeyed Naomi's charge to stay with her sister, Orpah, in Moab, but now she does everything her mother-in-law asks.

At Naomi's bidding, she goes to Boaz's fields to harvest grain. The Levitical laws required landowners to leave the edges of their fields for the poor to harvest.[1] Boaz is a just man. He not only complies, but also blesses the reapers. Ruth's peace, shown in her obedience to Naomi, makes for justice.

Ruth obeys Naomi's further direction to go to the threshing room floor at night even though it clearly places her in a compromising situation with Boaz (3:6-18). Scholars argue that Naomi sets up a potential seduction. She hopes to get Ruth pregnant by the sated Boaz, but it is not clear what happens between Ruth and Boaz that night. What is clear is that Boaz seeks justice immediately. The next morning, he sets out to rectify the dead Elimelech's estate by speaking with Elimelech's kin. In public and at the city gates, he asks for Elimelech's property, which includes Ruth. He declares his intention to make Ruth his wife, and he calls on the townspeople to witness the transaction. Again, Ruth's peace makes for justice. In Ruth's story, the psalmist's prediction literally comes true: "Love and truth will meet; justice and peace will kiss" (Psalm 85:11, NAB).

Bringing a Sword; Being Peace

With her husband, Boaz, Ruth has a child, and the final scene in Ruth's story shows Naomi holding her newborn grandson, Obed. No longer Mara, meaning "bitter," Naomi takes up her old name. She returns to blessing. The book of Ruth ends with a genealogy that traces Obed's line to David.

If the lineage sounds familiar, this is because Matthew repeats it at the beginning of his Gospel. There, Ruth's story stands out. Matthew's list of Joseph's ancestors is overwhelmingly male and highly unpronounceable, all of which serves to make us notice the interruptions. Some in the genealogy are women, and many of the women are foreigners: Tamar, a woman who sought justice and found it; Rahab, a Canaanite woman and liberator of the Jews; Bathsheba, probably a Hittite woman, whom David widowed and then married himself; and Mary, pregnant out of wedlock. Then there is Ruth, the Moabite woman.

In Jesus' genealogy, kings stand alongside their sworn enemies, Canaanites and Moabites. Women who stood for peace and struggled for justice are featured with warriors and soldiers. Ancient enemies become kin in Jesus. And, all of the bloodlines arc forward to a manger in Naomi's hometown, to a child in Bethlehem whom Isaiah named the "Prince of Peace." In Jesus, justice and peace have kissed.

Yet, at times, Jesus seems not so much a peacemaker as a peacebreaker. He sends the twelve apostles out with some sobering instructions.

> Do not think that I have come to bring peace to the earth; I have not come to bring peace, but a sword.
>> For I have come to set a man against his father,
>>> and a daughter against her mother,
>>> and a daughter-in-law against her mother-in-law;
>>> and one's foes will be members of one's own household.
> (Matthew 10:34-36)

Had Ruth listened to Jesus' instruction, she may well have stayed in Moab. Yet, if we understand what Jesus says here, we must revere Ruth as a disciple before her time. She rightly deserves a place in Jesus' genealogy because early on, she recognizes the new family God creates—and she wants to become part of it.

Many celebrations of Christian marriage use the passage from Ruth where the Moabite woman declares her devotion to her mother-in-law. It is interesting that we ignore the fact that Naomi did not really want company on her return trip and that she seemed too self-absorbed to notice anyone's devotion. Yet, considering the toll that narcissism, rejection, and emotional distance take on a marriage, these words might be all too apt.

But, Ruth is not declaring her devotion just to Naomi. She redefines family ties to mean the family of the children of God: "Your people shall be my people, and your God my God" (Ruth 1:16). With these words, she joins a new family that is not Naomi's alone.

Ruth's words see into the future, predicting the implications of Christian baptism. For in this rite, Christians are taken from their families of origin and are joined to the family of the children of God. Too often, we mistake baptism for christening, as if the most important name conferred upon an infant is its family name: Rosa Catherine *Stortz* or Mary Elizabeth *Wolff*. But, baptism and christening could not be further apart.

With baptism, we receive a new identity, one that does not come with a passport or identification card, but with relationships. New relationships replace the old ones. In Matthew's Gospel, Jesus states the matter dramatically. A sword severs the old ties between blood relatives. Baptism is stronger than blood.

Of course, Christian baptism was not an option for Ruth. Still, her new family replaced her old one. Ruth left behind her Moabite kin and joined herself to Naomi's family. More importantly, she left behind her Moabite gods and joined herself to Naomi's God. This gave her a new identity.

In baptism, *who* we are depends decisively on *whose* we are. The apostle Paul puts these new relationships simply and powerfully: "You belong to Christ, and Christ belongs to God" (1 Corinthians 3:23). These relationships shape baptismal identity as God adopts us into the family of the children of God. Living into these relationships, we live into the world according to God. Ruth may be the first Moabite, that is, "Child of God," and in so becoming, she embodies the promise of this beatitude: "Blessed are the peacemakers, for they will be called children of God."

Baptismal ceremonies repeat ancient gestures of adoption, which Moabite and Hebrew alike would have recognized. In the ancient world, lifting up a newborn was a way of claiming the child as a member of the family. Immediately after birth, an infant was presented to the child's presumptive father, and he could choose to lift the child up or not. In lifting up the child, a father claimed paternity, and the claimed child would rest secure in the family's embrace and inheritance.

Unfortunately, not all newborns were so claimed. Children were routinely set down to die of exposure or to be picked up by others. The public squares of Greco-Roman cities had a spot, the *lactarium*, where such unclaimed children were customarily abandoned. They could be picked up by strangers and raised as slaves, servants, or prostitutes. Sometimes they were picked up by childless families and adopted as sons and daughters, heirs to the family fortune.[2]

Ancient practices of adoption stand as a backdrop for Christian baptism. Then and now, new Christians are adopted into a new family in baptism. They are ceremonially lifted up and claimed as children of God. The apostle Paul alludes to these ancient practices in his discussion of baptism:

> For you did not receive a spirit of slavery to fall back into fear, but you have received a spirit of adoption. When we cry, "Abba! Father!" it is that very Spirit bearing witness with our spirit that we are children of God, and if children, then heirs, heirs of God and joint heirs with Christ—if, in fact, we suffer with him so that we may also be glorified with him. (Romans 8:15-17)

What are the family values of the children of God? Peace and justice. Ruth embodies both. She makes peace between two warring peoples, and in so doing, she restores broken relationships. In the family of the children of God, "justice and peace will kiss."

Jesus Bears Reconciliation

Peace is Jesus' deepest desire for all of his disciples. He lives out that longing. He searches out his disciples after the resurrection even though they had betrayed and deserted him. The disciples yearn for Jesus; they also fear him. His death brought out their worst selves. Peter denied Jesus three times, and any one of them could have said what Peter did. Because they did not claim Jesus, they wonder if he will still claim them. Having renounced their identity as Jesus' disciples, they no longer know who they really are. They have no identity. As John's Gospel tells the story, after they hear rumors of a resurrection, the disciples huddle in terror behind locked doors, lest Jewish or Roman authorities find them and subject them to Jesus' fate.

Suddenly, Jesus is in their midst. Before anyone says a word, Jesus speaks: "Peace be with you." He has to repeat it twice more before the disciples can calm down (John 20:19, 21, 26). In every encounter, Jesus brings his disciples peace. The resurrected Christ speaks the wisdom of the dead: "Rest in peace."

That peace is hard to find in our warlike world. Israel and Palestine wrestle over yet another peace process. Wars in Iraq and Afghanistan have failed to bring peace or even democracy. A body of "united nations" pleads for peace among its unruly members. Yet, finally, peace is not a process, nor a place, nor a plea, but a person. Jesus Christ is the Prince of Peace. When peace comes to us as a person, all we have to do is follow.

Family Values among the Children of God

Where does following a Prince of Peace lead us? A church in the Pacific Northwest answered this question in its mission statement: "Gathered to worship; scattered to serve." Through baptism, they live out family values among the children of God: making peace and doing justice.

For Christians, baptism is both event and practice, both a onetime rite and a lifetime calling. We take seriously the hands-on gestures of the onetime event. Baptism makes us part of a new family of the children of God. We also take seriously the hands-on gestures of the lifetime calling. Baptism makes us Christ's hands in the world, as we scatter to embrace all of God's children.

Family values among the children of God are clear: make peace and do justice. We bring those values to bear on relationships both inside and outside our immediate family. Inside the family, baptism gathers Christians into a new family of the children of God. Because baptism incorporates us into the body of the Prince of Peace, we are empowered to be princes and princesses of peace in a world bent on war.

What does this mean concretely? It means making peace and doing justice among ourselves. Not only do I get to share the peace of Christ with people I do not like or with people who do not like me, but also I am charged to make peace with them. I am charged to see that my relationships are right. Sometimes this involves the kind of disobedience Ruth showed Naomi in Moab when she refused to obey her mother-in-law's command to stay put. Sometimes this involves the kind of obedience Ruth showed Naomi in Bethlehem. Obedience to God's *shalom* is never blind. It always invites us to "listen for" God's call: literally, *ob-* + *-audire*, "to hear from."

Baptism defines a dangerous community. Paul described that community to the Galatians: "There is no longer Jew or Greek, there is no longer slave or free, there is no longer male and female; for all of you are one in Christ Jesus" (Galatians 3:28). In Christ, traditional boundaries vanish, and Christians practice a new form of community that cuts across the boundaries of family and tribe, race and nationality, class and gender. In the movie *Romero*, a wealthy young woman asks Archbishop Oscar Romero of San Salvador to baptize her daughter in a private ceremony. Romero politely refuses, saying that baptisms must be performed at the Sunday liturgy when all the faithful are present. The mother looks worried and then blurts out, "But I don't want my daughter baptized with all those Indians!" She did not understand family values among the children of God. Baptism creates a dangerous community where rich and poor, white and black, brown and red are brothers and sisters. In baptism, we enter into the wild joy of all the children of God.

This new community of brothers and sisters in Christ has responsibilities outside the immediate family. It is not enough—it has never been enough—just to take care of family. As Christ's body in the world, baptized Christians may be the only way many people encounter Jesus. We may be their call to "follow me." As members of the body, we proclaim God's love to a world that is hungry for it.

Too often, Christians display baptism as a badge of privilege, as if our cherished identity singles us out as the *only* beloved children of God. This understanding of baptism could not be further from the truth. In fact, by incorporating Christians into the body of the Prince of Peace, baptism drafts us as witnesses to God's *shalom* for the whole world. Disciples continue the incarnation by embodying God's peace for the whole world.

What does this mean concretely? It means making peace and doing justice in the world. The Great Judgment of Matthew 25 tells us everything we need to know: food for the hungry, drink for the thirsty, welcome to the stranger, clothes for the naked, care for the sick, comfort to those in prison. These last words in Jesus' public ministry echo his first words, the beatitudes. Only now, Jesus himself has become the one who is poor in spirit, mournful, meek, and hungry for righteousness. The disciples are amazed: "When was it that we saw you?" they ask. Jesus replies, "Just as you did it to one of the least of these who are members of my family, you did it to me" (Matthew 25:31-46). Unaware, the disciples have been swept up into God's *shalom*.

But, the Great Judgment does not end there. Jesus names our failures: "For I was hungry and you gave me no food, I was thirsty and you gave me nothing to drink." When we fail to make peace and do justice, the best that disciples can do is repent and celebrate those places where peace and justice kiss, whether that passionate embrace involves Christians or not. Sometimes the Prince of Peace works outside the immediate family because his brothers and sisters are too busy squabbling over a building project or carping at the altar guild or admiring their lovely new vestments or just being spiritual couch potatoes.

In these moments, we can only thank God that there is extended family around. Sometimes we depend on outsiders to point us toward the pathways of peace. God brings *shalom* because of and in spite of us. Here, the fecklessness of the original disciples ought to give us pause. We repent to remember that too often the people who really "got" God's peace were not in the immediate family, such as a centurion at the foot of the cross (Mark 15:39), the blind Bartimaeus (Mark 10:47), a Roman centurion with a sick slave (Luke 7:2-10), a Syrophoenician/Canaanite woman (Mark 7:25-30; Matthew 15:21-28)—even a Moabite woman named Ruth.

Questions for Reflection

1. Is Ruth's story really the shift from political to personal that it seems to be? Its placement between Judges and 1 Samuel suggests that the book has political import as well. The story falls in a time of civil unrest. Everyone in Israel did "what was right in their own eyes" (Judges 21:25). Does that feel like the situation today? Does the book of Ruth have anything to say to us?

2. Think about the family values of your own families, your congregation, and our country. What are they? How do we live them out?

3. Think about the family values for the family of the children of God? What would you add to the two identified here: justice and peace? How are they lived out?

4. Have you ever risked disobedience in the name of peace or justice? Were there consequences? How did you know you were working for God's peace?

For Further Reflection

Psalm 85

Here, a people acknowledge the consequences of wrongdoing. Bad faith has broken the relationship with their God, and they can no longer bear the distance they have created between themselves and God. They can no longer stand the anger they have provoked and the conflict they have caused. They long for what they have squandered: divine *shalom*. The language of their lament says it all: "Restore us, revive us, and return to us your favor." The psalm ends with a beautiful vision of that lost peace:

> Steadfast love and faithfulness will meet;
>   righteousness and peace will kiss each other.
> Faithfulness will spring up from the ground,
>   and righteousness will look down from the sky.
> The LORD will give what is good,
>   and our land will yield its increase.
> Righteousness will go before him,
>   and will make a path for his steps. (vv. 10-13)

God answered the people's lament not with a word, but with a person, Jesus Christ, Son of God, Prince of Peace.

9

Blessings in the Midst of Suffering

Blessed are those who are persecuted for righteousness' sake, for theirs is the kingdom of heaven.

—Matthew 5:10

A retired teacher wrote of her struggle with cancer. In the long, sleepless nights before her first operation, she wrestled fiercely with God. Then she heard the voice that prophets and apostles throughout the centuries have heard: "It is I; be not afraid." She wrote: "And as I lay there listening to those words, I suddenly became aware in a most remarkable way that this gentle offer of support was coming from the middle of my cancer, from the very center of the malignancy. *'It is I. Be not afraid. I am here too. I am not only in the daytime, and the color and the safety of the three-dimensional world that you are seeking. I am here at the center of all that you most fear. There is no otherness. It is I.'*"[1]

On the night of November 16, 1989, a Salvadoran Army patrol murdered six Jesuit priests, their housekeeper, and her fourteen-year-old daughter at the university in San Salvador. The priests were advocates for human rights in El Salvador, and the women cooked and cleaned for them. When outsiders were allowed into the site of the mass murder, they found Father Ignacio Martin-Baro's blood spattered all over the book he had been reading when the soldiers entered the compound: *The Crucified God*, by German theologian Jürgen Moltmann.[2]

Both of these stories testify to the living presence of a suffering God. God became one of us in order to experience everything we experience, even suffering and persecution. In this final beatitude we meet the crucified God, the God at the center of all that we most love and all that we most fear. The psalmist writes of God's bounty in the midst of enemy attack, and the apostle Paul writes of endurance in the midst of persecution. Both offer insight into a God who suffers with us.

The Mystery of God's Bounty

"How could God let something like this happen?" Again and again the question comes, and I have no answers. My neighbor lost her husband at the age of sixty-five. They were poised for a golden retirement, with grandchildren to spoil together and travels to take together. Illness and death erased all of that.

Her husband and my own were diagnosed with brain cancer within months of each other. Throughout their illnesses, we shared doctors and treatments, home remedies and information on clinical trials around the country. The four of us would go out to dinner together, booking a booth so that whoever had the more recent surgery could hide his scars. Treatments worked for her husband that did not work for mine and vice versa. We knew eventually that nothing would work. Still, we had each other, and we grew closer through it all.

It could have been so different. Competition and secrecy could have shadowed our paths; we could have hoarded counsel or advice. We could have averted our eyes on the street, denying the truth unfolding in our midst. We could have lied, putting on a brave face for the sake of the other. Instead, we just kept having dinners, sharing stories— and laughing a lot. "I can't tell anyone else this—no one else would understand," she would exclaim. I felt the same way. Their presence was grace.

My husband died first. I sent his fleece pajamas across the street. In return, casseroles poured into my kitchen. Every so often I found flowers on my doorstep. They were from her—for no particular reason. Their ministry to me continued: a tiny miracle. They were looking at their own future. They knew it, and I knew it.

Now we two women eat alone together. I will cook, or she will cook. Neither of us is ready for the booth at the restaurant. Nor is the restaurant crowd ready for our tears and our dark humor. "How could God let something like this happen?" I have no answers, so I just listen.

But a line from Psalm 27 keeps running through my head: "I believe that I shall see the goodness of the Lord in the land of the living" (v. 13). I have seen that goodness: our neighbors revealed it. Their unfailing kindness delivered the bounty of the Lord to my doorstep. I have told her that.

Still, the question keeps coming: "How could God let something like this happen?" Maybe my attempt at an answer does not make sense, or maybe it does not make sense *yet*. In the meantime the only thing to do is to be together in our sorrow, as God has been with us.

Whistling in the Dark

My father was a great whistler, and he could do hymns, classical music, show tunes, anything. My sister and I wanted to whistle like that too. We would purse our lips and puff, usually producing more sputtering than sound, but gradually, we got better. In time we could do two-part, and then three-part harmony for a lot of those fine old Lutheran hymns we sang in the junior choir—at least until we all cracked up with the giggles.

Our family went camping one weekend, and my father led us to the bathrooms before lights-out. The night was dark, and the way was long. My sister and I convinced ourselves that the forest was full of bears. Nothing my father said could persuade us otherwise, so he gave up and started whistling. We could not resist joining in, shakily at first, then with more confidence. Before long, our fear of bears vanished.

Whistling in the dark is clearly the soundtrack for this Psalm 27. Despite the comfort of verse 13, "I believe that I shall see the goodness of the Lord in the land of the living," there is not much evidence of consolation in the rest of the psalm. Enemies abound, exposure threatens, and the psalmist longs for a safe haven. When the psalmist says, "I will sing and make melody to the Lord," he signals that he is in a darkness that threatens to swallow all sound. The psalm is an attempt to whistle in the dark, and its song comforts us as we face our own dark nights and gloomy days.

Why Do You Persecute Me?

The apostle Paul faced an unwelcome darkness. As Saul, he persecuted Christians, authorizing the stoning of Stephen, the first Christian martyr, and guarding the coats of an angry mob. The author of Luke and Acts reports tersely, "And Saul approved of their killing him. That day a severe persecution began against the church in Jerusalem" (Acts 8:1). Then a blinding vision knocked Saul off his horse, and Jesus asked him, "Why do you persecute me?" (Acts 9:3-4).

Following this encounter on the Damascus road, Saul had plenty of time to ponder the stunning reversal that left him, the persecutor, blind, helpless, and left alone among the very people he persecuted. In those dark hours, he gave himself over to prayer. As a good Pharisee, he probably had all the psalms written on his heart. Perhaps he even prayed Psalm 27, hoping wildly to see "the goodness of the Lord in the land of the living." But I imagine he would have settled for just seeing anything.

When the scales fell from his eyes, did Saul then see "the goodness of the Lord?" His eyes focused on the face of Ananias, the disciple who restored his sight. Three days before, Saul had sought to kill such a man who now had healed him. Now this former persecutor of the disciples of Jesus joined the disciples. When word of Saul's conversion leaked out, the disciples in Damascus smuggled Saul out of harm's way. Saul became Paul, persecutor turned preacher of the Risen Christ. It is the most stunning reversal of all.

Later in his ministry, Paul made a song of his own story, chronicling all the incredible reversals that make up the journey of discipleship. He sang it to the community in the city of Corinth, a cosmopolitan city full of pagan customs, charismatic prophets, and sages of all stripes. Paul deflated their smugness with irony. Imagine music in his words, and whistle along, if you dare:

> For I think that God has exhibited us apostles as last of all, as though sentenced to death, because we have become a spectacle to the world, to angels and to mortals. We are fools for the sake of Christ, but you are wise in Christ. We are weak, but you are strong. You are held in

honor, but we in disrepute. To the present hour we are hungry and thirsty, we are poorly clothed and beaten and homeless, and we grow weary from the work of our own hands. When reviled, we bless; when persecuted, we endure; when slandered, we speak kindly. We have become like the rubbish of the world, the dregs of all things, to this very day. (1 Corinthians 4:9-13)

Then Paul chided the proud Corinthians: "I am not writing this to make you ashamed, but to admonish you as my beloved children . . . for the kingdom of God depends not on talk but on power. What would you prefer? Am I to come to you with a stick, or with love in a spirit of gentleness?" (1 Corinthians 4:14, 20-21). Like the schoolteacher in her cancer and Father Martin-Baro in his book, Paul found the goodness of the Lord in the midst of persecution. Only a crucified God can help.

The Goodness of the Lord

"Begin and end each day with beauty," a friend urges. She keeps a stack of art books by her bedside. She is newly ninety, as she puts it, full of wonder and elegant as ever. She moves more slowly now with the aid of an ivory-handled cane: "Sometimes it's my third eye—and sometimes it's my third leg." I want to grow up to be like her. If I thought I had half a chance, I would start buying those thick coffee-table volumes now.

But poetry is my passion, so I read poems before sleeping and psalms upon waking. I figure that if I let the Lord "open my lips," other lyrics can close them down. Whether biblical or lyrical, poetry works for me the way images work for my friend. We are both taking time to rest in the goodness of the Lord.

The truth, though, is that beauty is not enough. Suffering and persecution dull the senses. The world takes on the color of terror; beauty is the last thing we look for when we are in mortal pain or when death squads storm the gates. That is why God sent goodness to our doorstep, the goodness whose name is Jesus. The God born in Bethlehem came to live through the full range of human experience, especially, it seems, the experience of those who suffer and those who are persecuted.

Jesus spent much of his time with people who were suffering or persecuted. He healed lepers, and leprosy was an ugly, disfiguring disease (see Luke 17:11-19). Risking not only ritual impurity, but also contraction of the disease itself, Jesus touched the lepers to heal them (see Mark 1:40-45; Matthew 8:1-4; Luke 5:12-16).

Demonic possession did not frighten Jesus either. Rather, he frightened the demons. When they saw him coming, these ambassadors of evil fled in terror. They knew without doubt that the goodness of the Lord had appeared in their midst, and they protested fiercely. "What have you to do with us, Jesus of Nazareth? Have you come to destroy us? I know who you are, the Holy One of God," one blurted before fleeing (Mark 1:23-28).[3] In another encounter an evil spirit had driven a Gerasene man to the edges of human society. Filthy and shackled, he lived among the dead. Jesus scolded the spirits, beckoning them out of the man. The demons knew exactly what they were up against: the goodness of the Lord. "What have you to do with me, Jesus, Son of the Most High God? I adjure you by God, do not torment me" (Mark 5:7).

Blood could not blot out the goodness of the Lord. Despite the laws that labeled those with open wounds and flowing blood as impure people, Jesus allowed himself to be touched by a woman who had been bleeding for twelve years (Mark 5:25-34). He blessed her, claimed her as a child of God, and sent her forth into a peace she had not known for years.

Even death did not deter Jesus. Contact with a corpse contaminated people even more than blood, tarnishing their righteousness. Jesus brought God's goodness not just *to* the grave, but also *into* and *through* the grave. Disregarding the law, he touched Jairus' daughter, bringing her back to life (Mark 5:22-24, 35-43). At the sound of his voice, Lazarus emerged from his tomb (John 11:1-44).

But Jesus not only spent time with the unloved and the unlovely; he became one of them himself. He not only brought the goodness of the Lord into the land of suffering and persecution; he took all of this evil upon himself, leaving us only blessing in return. Martin Luther called this "the happy exchange" (*Froehliche Wechsel*).

The Great Judgment or the Great Promise?

Scholars call Jesus' last sermon in the Gospel of Matthew the Great Judgment. They read the sermon from a *hermeneutics of narcissism*, as if the Bible were all about *us*. In this reading, the Great Judge separates the sheep from the goats and sends the sheep off into eternal life and the goats into eternal punishment. This reading sees ourselves as the sheep, of course. It is all about us.

This interpretation misses the point of Jesus' last sermon. Listen to this sermon from another angle, a *hermeneutics of goodness*, for the Bible too is full of "the goodness of the Lord." In this reading, Jesus makes a promise, not just a judgment. He shows the astonished herd of sheep and goats that he has been with the hungry, the thirsty, the stranger, the naked, the sick, and the imprisoned. Not only has he been *with* them, he has been *one of them*. He tells the sheep and goats again and again, "Just as you did it to one of the least of these . . . you did it to *me*" (emphasis added). Jesus has absorbed suffering, persecution, and death into his own body.

In this reading, Jesus' last sermon becomes a story of the Great Promise: the promise of Emmanuel, which means, "God is with us." The retired schoolteacher discovered this truth as she faced her cancer. Father Martin-Baro realized this truth as he faced his murderers. It is the truth of a God who became one of us to shoulder our suffering and to participate in our persecution.

Nobel Prize winning author and concentration camp survivor Elie Wiesel tells a riveting story of an execution of several prisoners, one of them a young boy, at a Nazi concentration camp.[4] As the floor falls away under their feet, the men drop and die. Their weight on the nooses snaps their necks instantly. The boy, however, is not heavy enough for the noose to do its deadly work quickly. He struggles against gravity, slowly strangling. The crowd watches in horror, and one of the spectators asks, "Where is God now?" Wiesel relates that he heard a voice within him answer, "Where is He? Here He is—He is hanging here on this gallows. . . ."

We who dwell here know to our cost that "the land of the living" is full of pain. We cling all the more fiercely to the promise of a God who absorbed the world's pain on the cross and left us with the goodness of abundant life. The crucified God promises resurrection.

Disciples As "The Least of These"

Twelve-Step programs do not work because of the steps, but because of the stories. Few people stop drinking or drugging or enabling because someone said "Stop!" Instead, they get the point from someone else's story.

Stories are at the heart of recovery. At every meeting, someone opens with a brief autobiography: how she fell into her addiction, how she hit bottom and what the bottom was like, and how she came back to wholeness. No judgment and no cross talk are allowed. Listeners respond by telling a story or two of their own. People recognize themselves in these stories of despair and redemption: "I've been there too." "Maybe I could do that too." Then the steps come into play, helping people turn their lives into stories of blessing and sharing that blessing with others.

The ancient world did not have Twelve-Step programs, but it had stories. The prophet Nathan told one to David (2 Samuel 12:1-15). It is a story about a poor man and a rich man. The rich man, who has many flocks and herds, steals the poor man's beloved and only lamb for a tasty meal. The story draws David in, but he identifies with the wrong person. David righteously condemns the greedy rich man: he deserves to die. Then Nathan shifts from third-person narration to second-person accusation: "*You* are the man!" (emphasis added) David has judged himself.

In similar fashion, the beatitudes draw the disciples in. Jesus describes a world turned upside-down. Conditions that the world judges as accursed become occasions of blessing: the poor in spirit will gain the kingdom of heaven; the pure in heart will see God; those who mourn will be comforted; the meek will inherit the earth; and so on. The first four beatitudes address victims of the world's ways; the second four address those who aid them. All of these people will be richly blessed.

Read again the first eight beatitudes, which bless in third-person plural ("they" and "those") the people who suffer along with those who aid them. Listen to the cadence of blessing, the beauty of language. We would all like to see a world like that.

With the ninth beatitude, however, Jesus turns to directly address those to whom he is speaking. He speaks to disciples using the word *you*. The blessings refer to *them*; the promises tell *their* future. They are not just spectators watching as the world turns; they do the turning. Remember the cartoon character Pogo, who looked at his friends and wailed, "We have met the enemy—and he is us!" Jesus' first sermon is similar: "We have met the blessed, and *they* are us!"

Not only will Jesus take the world's pain into his own body, but so will all who follow him. Like Jesus, disciples will become "the least of these," as they suffer and aid those who suffer and as they are persecuted and aid those who are persecuted.

But here is the promise: suffering and persecution will not be the last words. The first eight beatitudes begin and end with the same promise: the kingdom of heaven. The final beatitude, addressed directly to the disciples, spells this out: "Rejoice and be glad, for your reward is great in heaven." In God's kingdom, the goodness of the Lord reigns fully and completely, and every tear will be wiped away.

Works of Mercy; Responses to Blessing

A young man approached the bishop of Seattle and asked, "What must I do to become a Christian?" Do you remember the good bishop's answer? "Go to Mass every Sunday and work in a soup kitchen every week." It is a wise answer because if Christianity is about following Jesus, would-be disciples need to know where to find him. We meet Jesus as we gather around Word and Sacrament; we meet him in those who suffer and face persecution. It is worth noting that in both settings, his body is broken. In the Lord's Supper, it is broken for us so that it can become our food and so that we can be knit together into one body. In suffering, that body is broken in the shattered bodies and spirits of those who are persecuted. In and through that brokenness, Jesus promises the goodness of God for the land of the living. The final beatitude suggests two practices of discipleship: the Lord's Supper and the "works of mercy" outlined in Jesus' last sermon.

Living into Blessing

If someone wants directions to my house, I ask which route they prefer: the direct route or the scenic route. The scenic route takes the long, hilly way around, but the view is worth it. The direct route is your basic freeway. You do not get the view, but you get where you are going—fast. The actions outlined in Jesus' last sermon give the direct route to disciples then and now. "If you want to find me, this is where to look," Jesus seems to be saying. Look to where people are suffering and persecuted.

But discipleship is no spectator sport. The beatitudes did not bless disciples just so that we would *look* good; they bless us to *do* good. When we do good, we are not bearing our own goodness, but the goodness of the Lord. Through that goodness, broken for us in the Lord's Supper, we become what we eat. As Luther put it, we bear the face of Christ to our neighbor. We are blessed to be a blessing. Jesus is quite specific about the good that we do: feed the hungry; give the thirsty something to drink; welcome the stranger; clothe the naked; care for the sick; and visit the prisoners. Jesus' counsel is concise, direct, and urgent.

Our Roman Catholic brothers and sisters add two other acts, sheltering the homeless and burying the dead, and they call all of these actions the seven corporal works of mercy. This language alarms Lutherans because it seems to support "works righteousness." Luther insisted that we cannot—and we need not—earn our blessing. We need to remember that the disciples in question have already been blessed—blessed to be a blessing. The beatitudes already gave disciples both blessing and promise. All we have to do is say "yes." These actions tell us how we are to respond to the blessing we have already received. Through them, we bring the goodness of the Lord into the land of the living.

Questions for Reflection

1. Has someone you know (maybe even you) ever asked God, "How could you let something like this happen?" What were the circumstances? Was there a response? Was it the response that was expected?

2. Can you recount a time when you entered dark days? Did you believe you would ever see your way to find the goodness of the Lord? Maybe you are still in the dark and have not whistled yourself out of it yet. What is going on?

3. Have you (or someone you know) found the goodness of the Lord in the land of suffering? If so, where? How? In whom?

4. Paul's song describes the world according to God. Does it sound inviting? Why or why not? If your congregation had a theme song, what would it be?

5. Saul, the persecutor, becomes Paul, the persecuted. This is a stunning reversal. Have you seen or experienced such a reversal in your own life?

6. Have you recognized Jesus in your own suffering or the suffering of someone else? How did you recognize him?

For Further Reflection

Psalm 33

The psalmist declares that "the earth is full of the goodness of the Lord" (v. 5, KJV)—and he is not kidding around. God's goodness has personal and political dimensions. The righteous people, along with righteous nations, are swept up in the goodness of the Lord. Interestingly, that goodness may be more a matter of conviction than present reality. The psalmist makes allusion to famine, death, and a king's mighty army even as he declares his commitment to wait on the Lord. The psalm ends in hope: "Let your steadfast love, O Lord, be upon us, even as we hope in you" (v. 22). The words pulse with movement, describing an eternal circle of blessing. God's love descends to rest upon the people who long for justice, even as they place their hope in the Lord. Let it be so!

Notes

Introduction: Called by Blessing

1. Martin Luther, "The Small Catechism," in *The Book of Concord*, ed. Theodore G. Tappert (Philadelphia: Fortress Press, 1959), 343-344.

2. Martin Luther, "A Brief Instruction on What to Look for and Expect in the Gospels," *Luther's Works*, vol. 35, American Edition, ed. E. Theodore Buchmann (Philadelphia: Fortress Press, 1960), 117-118.

3. Martin Luther, "The Sermon on the Mount," *Luther's Works*, vol. 21, American Edition, ed. Jaroslav Pelikan (St. Louis: Concordia, 1956), 111-114.

4. Ibid., 27-30.

5. Sermon on Matt. 21:1-9 (Weimar Ausgabe, Vol. X-I-1, p. 626); on this passage and on "the Word of God" in Luther generally see Jaroslav Pelikan, *From Luther to Kierkegaard* (St. Louis: Concordia, 1950), 18-19; *Luther the Expositor: Introduction to the Reformer's Exegetical Writings* (St. Louis: Concordia, 1959), 63-65.

Chapter 1: Count Your Blessings; Hold Fast to the Promise

1. Saint Augustine, *Confessions* 1.1, trans. Henry Chadwick (New York: Oxford University Press, 1991), 3.

2. View these paintings online at the Web Gallery of Art: www.wga.hu/

3. Scripture texts from the *Holy Bible, New International Version®*, copyright © 1973, 1978, 1984 International Bible Society. Used by permission of Zondervan Publishing House. All rights reserved.

The "NIV" and "New International Version" trademarks are registered in the United States Patent and Trademark Office by International Bible Society. Use of either trademark requires the permission of International Bible Society.

Chapter 2: Poor in Spirit; Rich in Blessing

1. Martin Luther, "The Large Catechism," in *The Book of Concord*, ed. Theodore Tappert (Philadelphia: Fortress Press, 1959), 365.

2. The full text of Luther's note is quoted in Heiko Oberman, *Luther: Man between God and the Devil*, trans. Eileen Walliser-Schwarzbart (New Haven, Conn.: Yale University Press, 1989), 166.

3. In conceiving a child, Hannah joins the mighty ranks of biblical women who conceive late in life: Sarah (Gen. 17:16-19); Rebekah (Gen. 25:21-26); Rachel (Gen. 30:22-23); the mother of Samson (Judg. 13:2-5); and Mary's cousin, Elizabeth (Luke 1:5-17).

Chapter 3: The Country of Mourning

1 Psalms 37 and 73 wrestle with this question, as do the prophets Jeremiah (12:1) and Habakkuk (1:4).

2. Scripture texts from *The New King James Version*, copyright © 1979, 1980, 1982 Thomas Nelson, Inc. Used by permission. All rights reserved.

3. The phrase is Wendell Berry's, and the poems describe the landscape of this country beautifully. Wendell Berry, *The Country of Marriage* (New York: Harcourt Brace Jovanovich, 1975).

4. Martin Luther, "Lectures on Genesis," *Luther's Works*, vol. 1, American Edition, ed. Jaroslav Pelikan (St. Louis: Concordia, 1958), 94.

Chapter 5: Follow Your Heart and Find the Heart of God

1. Saint Augustine, *Confessions*, 1.1, trans. Henry Chadwick (New York: Oxford University Press, 1998), 3.

2. Scripture texts from the *New American Bible*, copyright © 1970 by the Confraternity of Christian Doctrine, Washington, DC, are used by permission of the copyright owner. All rights reserved.

3. Bernard of Clairvaux, "On Loving God," in *Bernard of Clairvaux: Selected Writings/Western Classics of Spirituality*, trans. G. R. Evans (Mahwah, N.J.: Paulist, 1987), 173-206.

4. Martin Luther, "The Large Catechism," in *The Book of Concord*, ed. Theodore Tappert (Philadelphia: Fortress Press, 1959), 365.

5. So does the author of 1 John: "God's love was revealed among us in this way: God sent his only Son into the world so that we might live through him. In this is love, not that we loved God but that he loved us and sent his Son to be the atoning sacrifice for our sins." (4:9-10).

6. "All Praise to You, Eternal Lord," *Lutheran Book of Worship* (Minneapolis: Augsburg Fortress, 1978), #48.

7. Elizabeth Barrett Browning, *Sonnets from the Portuguese*, no. 43.

Chapter 6: Mercy Made Real

1. C. S. Lewis, *Letters to Malcolm: Chiefly on Prayer* (Mahwah, N.J.: Paulist, 1985), 106.

2. Luke 5:23 is one example of a Gospel story of healing that speaks simultaneously about forgiveness: "Which is easier, to say, 'Your sins are forgiven you,' or to say, 'Stand up and walk'?" Suddenly healed, the sick default to Peter's position. Blinded by the light of divine mercy, they can see only the familiar dirt of their own sinfulness. Jesus makes a preemptive strike: he forgives their sins before they can make Peter's speech. Finally, Jesus invites them to spread that mercy around.

Chapter 7: Pure in Heart; Rich in Vision

1. Saint Augustine, *Confessions*, 6.8, trans. Henry Chadwick (New York: Oxford University Press, 1991), 101.

2. Michael Ondaatje, *Anil's Ghost* (New York: Vintage Books/Random House, 2000).

3. The incident at Meribah is recorded twice, once in Exod. 17:1-7 and again in Num. 20:9-13. In the latter passage, the Lord charges Moses with taking credit for the miracle himself, rather than chalking it up to divine intervention. The cost is high: Moses cannot enter the promised land.

4. One of the great delights in medieval art comes from a misreading of the Hebrew *qaran* for "shining." Pointed differently, the word could also mean "horned" (*qeren*), and Moses often appears in medieval art with horns (see Michelangelo's sculpture in San Pietro in Vincoli in Rome). The iconography tested the limits of artistic imagination because the other great "horned" figure in Scripture was Satan. Artists struggled to depict Moses' headgear in a benevolent way—and Satan's more demonically. To see this image, go to www.artres.com and search Moses + statue + Michelangelo.

5. Remember the priest and the Levite in the parable of the Good Samaritan (Luke 10:31-32).

Chapter 8: Making Peace and Being Peace

1. Lev. 19:9-10; 23:22 and Deut. 24:19-22.

2. See John Boswell, *Kindness of Strangers: The Abandonment of Children in Western Europe from Late Antiquity to the Renaissance* (New York: Pantheon Books, 1988), 51-94; and Aline Rousselle, *Porneia: On Desire and the Body in Antiquity* (New York: Basil Blackwell, 1988), 47-62.

Chapter 9: Blessing in the Midst of Suffering

1. Margaret Roche Macey, "When Light Yields to Darkness: Facing the C Word," *America Magazine*, May 29, 2006: 22.

2. Jürgen Moltmann, *The Crucified God: The Cross of Christ as the Foundation and Criticism of Christian Theology* (London: SCM, 1974). For more information regarding the massacre, see the School of the Americas Watch Web site at http://www.soaw.org/new/article.php?id=44

3. Scholars think that utterances of demons and other supernatural beings could not be heard by mere humans. It was as if they spoke in a frequency outside the range of human hearing. Angels, however, seem to be able to make themselves understood: for example, Gabriel's conversation with Mary at the Annunciation (Luke 1:26-55); Zechariah's protest to an angel (Luke 1:10-20); the angelic chorus at Jesus' birth (Luke 2:8-20); and the angels' admonition to the disciples at the Ascension (Acts 1:11).

4. Elie Wiesel, *Night* (New York: Avon Books, 1969), 74-76.

For Further Reading

Dietrich Bonhoeffer. *Discipleship: Dietrich Bonhoeffer Works*, vol. 4, Geffrey B. Kelly and John D. Godsey, ed., Barbara Green and Reinhard Krauss, trans. Minneapolis: Fortress Press, 2001.

Dietrich Bonhoeffer. *Life Together and Prayerbook of the Bible: Dietrich Bonhoeffer Works*, vol. 5, Geffrey B. Kelly, ed., Daniel W. Bloesch and James H. Burtness, trans. Minneapolis: Fortress Press, 1996.

John R Donahue, *The Gospel in Parable: Metaphor, Narrative, and Theology in the Synoptic Gospels*. Minneapolis: Fortress Press, 1988.

Mary E. Hinkle. *Signs of Belonging: Luther's Marks of the Church and the Christian Life*. Minneapolis: Augsburg Fortress, 2003.

Ronald Rolheiser. *The Holy Longing: The Search for a Christian Spirituality*. New York: Doubleday, 1999.

Mark Allen Powell. *Loving Jesus*. Minneapolis: Fortress Press, 2004.

William C. Spohn. *Go and Do Likewise: Jesus and Ethics*. New York: Continuum, 1999.

Glen H. Stassen. *Living the Sermon on the Mount*. San Francisco: Jossey-Bass, 2006.

Martha Ellen Stortz. *A World According to God*. San Francisco: Jossey-Bass, 2004.